THE
POWER *of* RIGHT
THINKING

DESTINY IMAGE BOOKS BY KERRY KIRKWOOD

The Power of Imagination

The Power of Blessing

The Secret Power of Covenant

THE
POWER *of*
RIGHT THINKING

Transform Your Thoughts
Transform Your World

KERRY KIRKWOOD

DESTINY IMAGE® PUBLISHERS, INC.
P.O. Box 310, Shippensburg, PA 17257-0310
"Promoting Inspired Lives."
This book and all other Destiny Image and Destiny Image Fiction books are available at Christian bookstores and distributors worldwide.

Cover and interior design by Terry Clifton
For more information on foreign distributors, call 717-532-3040.
Reach us on the Internet: www.destinyimage.com.

ISBN 13 TP: 978-0-7684-0950-5
ISBN 13 eBook: 978-0-7684-0951-2

For Worldwide Distribution, Printed in the U.S.A.
2 3 4 5 6 7 8 / 20 19 18 17 16

DEDICATION

Everyone needs someone to be a champion of his or her life. I am thankful that I get to share life with my champion. My wife, Diane, has been that source of encouragement at all seasons of life. She has been a constant reminder of the promises God has so richly blessed our family with. When I laid down the idea of writing this book due to time obligations and life interruptions, it was my champion who pressed me to move forward with this message.

I will always be thankful for her input into every area of this book. She has reminded me at times of the thoughts that are attacking my judgment and she is there to help me pray through the process of getting the mind of the Lord. Everything I write has her touch on it. The legacy she gives to our four children and now six grandchildren is generational. She is a big part of what is imparted to our children. When I think of how God orchestrates the dynamic of a family, I am moved with emotion to know that God is in the center of everything we do. He is the Why, the What, and the How if we are willing to take the time to listen. This is where Diane shines by asking those three questions of Father God when we are needing to make decisions.

ACKNOWLEDGMENTS

I want to acknowledge the team that helps me daily and has been the proving ground of much of what is in this book. The staff and the elders of Trinity Fellowship Church in Tyler, Texas have been a great source of strength and encouragement. Duane Hett is the best executive pastor any pastor could hope for. He would take my visionary ideas and find a way to make them happen. Jim Hahn, our associate pastor, is one whom I leaned heavily upon to fill the speaking times while I was away. He and I have spent hours sharpening each other's gifting. Leah Brown, our worship pastor, is incredibly gifted and one of the easiest to work with when it comes to understanding our mission to worship extravagantly. Tina Smith, our office manager and fine arts director, is invaluable to our team. I mention their dedication because they have been with me for an average of 20 years. Anyone who has set out to accomplish tasks such as writing knows it takes a team to support and encourage the efforts of any project. I am eternally grateful for their collective support throughout the years.

CONTENTS

INTRODUCTION

Have you ever considered what it would be like if you could control your thoughts or choose to have God-like thoughts? Well, actually you can, and we will show you how. The world would certainly be a kinder and less violent environment to live in. Divorces would be diminished greatly. Wars would be infrequent, and best of all you and I would be more at peace than ever before.

The battle for the mind began in the Garden of Eden when a thought was introduced for the very first time. Satan, working through a serpent, injected the thought that God didn't really mean what He had said to Adam before Eve was taken out of Adam. God had instructed Adam that he was free to enjoy the garden and all of its fruit except the one tree that was deemed forbidden. It was called the Tree of Knowledge of Good and Evil. The Tree of Life was right there in the center of the garden, and it was not off-limits. The curiosity must have built until just a thought pushed Eve to the point of moving beyond the limits God had set. Eve even attempted to quote back to the serpent what God had said (see Genesis 3:3). The serpent flatly denied what God had said and then attempted to speak as one having authority:

> *You surely will not die! For God knows that in the day you eat from it your eyes will be opened, and you will be like God, knowing good and evil* (Genesis 3:4–5).

The serpent was saying, "You will be independent from God to make your own choices." This tree was rightly named the Tree of Knowledge of Good and Evil. It would open their thinking to mix good and evil. Before now, Adam and Eve were dominant in their spirit and less aware of their bodies. Once this tree of knowledge was introduced, they became dominant in their reasoning, which resulted in them becoming less dominant in their spirit and losing the glory of God and the ease with which they had communicated with God.

The enemy uses half-truths, twisting the thought processes to make us forget that we were created to fit God. Just one thought can change the destiny of an individual for better or worse. The power in that thought or suggestion can stay with a person until it eventually manifests into an action. Think how powerful it would be if one could control and direct their thinking in such a manner that it would align with God's intent and ultimately fulfill their potential.

> *For as he thinks within himself, so he is. He says to you, "Eat and drink!" But his heart is not with you* (Proverbs 23:7).

In this book you learn how to control thoughts that have created doubt and suspicion and reverse this by capturing the thoughts of God. Many have already seen their lives change through being able catch the thoughts of God and rule out the thoughts that do not build you as a person. You will be able to cleanse yourself from old replayed tapes that stop you from taking steps toward your God-given calling and potential. If we can change the way we think, we will never be defeated in life. If we can change the way we think about one another, we won't be ruled by the suspicion of what others think about us. If truth makes us free, then what would lies and wrong thinking do?

In this book you will discover that God has thoughts about you and those thoughts are prophetic downloads of potential. How we translate those thoughts into manifested reality is one of the keys you'll take away from reading this book. After 30 years of pastoral counseling I have discovered the vast majority of problems come from thoughts people harbor and consider to be either true or justified. Insecurity comes from not knowing the thoughts of God for my life and instead receiving thoughts that others have directly or indirectly fed into my thinking. Romans 12:2 teaches us that we are not to be conformed or fashioned by the world's system but instead be transformed through the renewing of our mind. Many have tried many different ways to change their lives only to find a pattern being repeated. Well, now you can learn how to detoxify your thinking, thus resulting in a mind makeover and a renewed life.

Part I

CONTROLLING YOUR THOUGHTS

Chapter 1

THE POWER OF RIGHT THINKING

For the weapons of our warfare are not carnal but mighty in God for pulling down strongholds, casting down arguments and every high thing that exalts itself against the knowledge of God, bringing every thought into captivity to the obedience of Christ (2 Corinthians 10:4–5 NKJV).

This book is not about perverted thoughts, pornographic thoughts—those kinds of things. Although these thoughts do exist, for most they usually pass quickly through our minds and are forgotten. Rather, I'm going to examine the everyday thoughts that most people have—thoughts that begin to build structures in our minds, for better or worse. Realizing the power of right thinking will make a tremendous difference in your life.

The Bible tells us in Ephesians 6:12 that our warfare is not against flesh and blood, but against principalities and powers in supernatural hierarchies. We are also told to cast out every thought that exalts itself above the knowledge of God. This is our litmus test for what thoughts we should allow into our minds and what thoughts should be pulverized. Thoughts we must immediately cast out are those that oppose the very nature of who God is.

We know that God is love. So God does not want us to entertain thoughts of revenge or anger toward another person. He does not want us to be excited when someone fails. He does not want us to be unforgiving, which ultimately causes our own doom. Having these thoughts doesn't make us bad people, but left in our minds to fester they can set in motion a multitude of actions that are not to our benefit.

Our thoughts should be of blessing as opposed to thoughts of cursing. The power of blessing means to see things the way God sees them and to see people the way God sees them. Thoughts of blessing are prophetic because they are viewing the value and potential that God sees in His creation. Blessing is much more than a salutation of "God bless you." It is thinking the way God thinks about ourselves and others.

This book focuses on the struggle in the area of thoughts and the life we create through thoughts. As we will see throughout this writing, thoughts create pictures and pictures can create destinies. The importance of right thinking is more than only having pure thoughts. It is about having thoughts that are in direct alignment with God's purpose. Romans 8:28

explains that all things work together collectively for my good because I am called to fulfill God's purpose. If I am not aware of the purpose of God, then my thoughts may be exploding in a million different directions and become confusing.

THE RIGHT MINDSET

I heard from a young lady in Abu Dhabi, a city located in the Middle East (sounds like a song in the '60s). She said, "I'm in a Muslim country here. I fear for my life. I'm confused about God. I thought God was love, but then I see where God is also a consuming fire. So I'm confused about who God is. God avenges and God kills and cuts out some and not others."

I told her gently, "The problem is you don't understand the principles of law and grace. You don't understand the loving grace of God. Jesus paid the price for all your sins. You're living in a covenant that He has fulfilled and completed." I tried to explain to her this concept, but her mind was so set on "I'm a bad person; God should punish me" that no matter how hard I worked at trying to describe God's grace and mercy, she just kept thinking that she would have to "pay the price."

"No, you don't," I told her. "Jesus paid the price, if you love Him with all of your heart and mind and strength. That's what He's called us to do." Her mindset would not let her hear what I was saying. Her thought life had built a structure that was resistant toward anything else entering into it. She had built a fortress out of her experiences and the thoughts she was taught growing up. She then applied those stronghold thoughts to God, and that brought the confusion of trying to accept the truth in grace while thinking about judgment and punishment.

Some people may have a stubborn view, which resists change and anything that would challenge previous thoughts. Their mind is made up about a certain subject or person or opinion, and it is like concrete—thoroughly mixed, poured, and set.

James describes this kind of thinking:

> *But he must ask in faith without any doubting, for the one who doubts is like the surf of the sea, driven and tossed by the wind. For that man ought not to expect that he will receive anything from the Lord,* **being a double-minded man, unstable in all his ways** *(James 1:6–8).*

Notice the connection between this man's thinking and his asking. He starts asking with thoughts of doubt, which is described as an unpredictable sea driven by what is happening with the wind at that moment. It is miserable to not be in control of your thoughts; one moment you are perfectly happy and blissful, then the wind changes in a moment and you are upset and defensive. What happened? When there is a double-minded structure in place there will be conflict. The Greek word for "double-minded" means "two spirited or two heads." The point that James makes is that when you are of two different minds, you never know which mind will rise up, and usually they are contrasting structures operating from past hurts or experiences.

In John 11, the story of Lazarus is recorded. When news was taken to Jesus concerning Lazarus being sick, Jesus said, "This sickness is not unto death" (John 11:4 KJV) and proceeded to stay two more days where He was. Jesus told the disciples with Him they were to go and awake Lazarus. Their thinking was that Lazarus was sleeping, not dead. The way Jesus thought and their thoughts were not aligned. Jesus was referring to resurrection. When Jesus arrived in Bethany, the common thought around Jesus was, "If you had been here, Lazarus would have not died." Can you see the difference of thought? Jesus had the thoughts of God, and Lazarus' family and friends could only think in terms of their experience. They had experience with Jesus healing but had not thought of raising someone from the dead. Jesus viewed Lazarus as in need of waking rather than dead. Due to their mental structure, they could not believe beyond their experience. Jesus had to convince them to remove the stone. All their minds could think of was how long he had been dead; the picture they had in their minds was gruesome. So we can see how thought affects what happens in the direction of our life.

Romans 12:2 instructs us that we can be transformed by the renewing of our mind. When we're born again, old things are passed away. I wish we were totally transformed on the day that we receive Christ, but that's just the beginning. Our continual transformation is the work of the Holy Spirit that starts us on a path to remove the brain fog and all the misconceptions we have of our heavenly Father. Transforming of our mind is a vital part of maturing and realizing the power in right thinking.

THE SCIENCE OF THOUGHT

I want to connect some science along with our biblical discussion. Have you ever heard of Dr. Caroline Leaf? She is a neuroscientist who wrote an excellent book, *Who Switched Off My Brain?* I read the book a few years ago, and recently I have been researching how the mind works, which has always intrigued me. This next section focuses on how creative God was when He crafted us—each of us is unique, yet there are similarities in the way males think and the way females think.

God designed us. We were created in the image of God. The word *image* is the Hebrew word *tselem,* which literally means "in the shadow of." So we are in the shadow of God— we are to resemble Him. We are to shadow Him. The purpose for someone to shadow another is to learn a new skill. Psalm 91:1–4 is a promise to those who will place themselves under His shadow. His shadow is much more than our concept of a shade. Normally when I think of a shadow I think of a giant oak tree that protects me from the harsh sun. *His shadow is actually His thoughts over us* (which you will see in more detail in later chapters), and when we learn to live under the shelter of His thoughts we have the promise of His shelter. It literally means I am abiding under the resemblance or the representation of God in me. The second verse of Psalm 91 calls the Lord "my refuge and my fortress." These two descriptive words used for being under His shadow/thoughts are distinct. *Refuge* is a word describing a shelter or a place of protective covering like a home. The word *fortress* in the Hebrew is a word meaning to capture, like a net would be used to capture prey. It implies an offensive posture toward one's enemies, whereas refuge is a defensive posture to be protected during a season of rest. The one who has learned how to live under this covering will be successful in taking new ground or holding existing ground. In either advancing or resting, God is still leading you into His purpose.

Dr. Leaf reveals fascinating aspects of this incredible part of us we call a brain. Now here's a few things to think about:

Every thought is made up of information and emotion, but it helps predict how we're going to react now and in the future because these thoughts connect. A thought from 20 years ago will connect with a current thought; the brain connects them. Some thoughts don't have any obvious connection. The thought of 20 years ago could be about abuse or rejection, and then all of a sudden a bad experience happens today and the brain connects the two and brings all those 20-year-old thoughts into the moment, building a bigger picture of the problem than what really exists. Isn't that interesting?

We react out of these building blocks we call thoughts. Proverbs 23:7 says that as a person thinks in his heart, so he becomes. If I'm not thinking correctly, I will not become what God intends me to be. If my mind is set on defending the way I have always thought about others and myself, then I won't be able to see through the lenses of God and see what He has in store for me.

The APG or "shifter" in the center of the brain, is larger in women than in men. This shifter is what allows us to move from one thought to the next. That's why women can be talking about something one moment and all of a sudden they are talking about something else, and we men are thinking, *Huh? I'm still over here talking about yesterday and you're talking about right now and I'm trying to catch up—wait for me!* Women are multitaskers; they move from one thing to the other as necessary at the moment. From getting the children ready for school to answering the phone to cleaning up after the dog to helping her husband find his socks—all within a half hour.

Dr. Leaf says that this shifting allows us to move between the left brain and the right brain. Feelings of emotion on the right side say, "I'm in love, I'm romantic, I love God, here's all my affection," then all of a sudden the left side of the brain declares, "I need to figure out the budget right now because the bills are due." Women have quicker shifters. That's why God says husbands are to dwell with them according to knowledge.

Men need to understand they are not going to rearrange a woman's shifter. She's got four in the floor and we're working on a two-speed. She can move from one emotion to another emotion quicker than men. Men will worry, but we're slower to get there. She'll tell you what you need to be worrying about, even to the point of saying, "I'm concerned that you're not bothered about what I'm bothered about." *Just give me a moment, I'll get there; I just need a moment process what you are saying.* Men process things in a different way than women do.

XX AND Y

A woman has two X chromosomes that allow her to see color and detail more distinctly than men. (Now some guys I know have an eye for color, but I'm not saying they have an extra X somewhere.) Women see details. For example, my wife, Diane, focuses on detail. "What flight are we on? When do we board? How will we get our rental car? Where's the hotel? How are we going to do that and get there?"

My response? "I don't know. I'm just going to show up and figure it out as I go along." She wants the details. And I've learned to let my Y connect with her double X and just somehow or another it works out. I see brown; Diane sees khaki.

Women are more prone to get stuck in shifting between left and right at some point and don't make transitions into the next. And men tend to get frustrated when we don't see them shifting with us. We're moving on. We've already made up our minds, but she's still shifting. So the point is, it's easy to get stuck in a thought or a moment and you don't want to move on. I need to solve this issue right here. Men will say, "Let it go." Women say, "I'm not letting it go, we need to deal with this right now." Men tend to procrastinate: "It will all work out." Women say, "We will work it out right now."

Women have more sensitivity receptors than men. They're sensitive over their entire body. I can't smell things; Diane has a stronger sense of smell. The house could be burning down and I wouldn't smell anything. Can you feel that fire? Yeah, all right, let's get out. God has created women with a higher sensitivity level to be touched. Men like to touch with their hands—a handshake is a good enough touch for them. We all need touch, but God created a woman's brain in such a way that she feels more secure when there's touch from someone she trusts.

Men are slightly bigger in the back of their brain. Women are a little larger in the front of the brain. And guess where the speech center is? You guessed it—in the front of the brain. Women are stimulated by conversation and most love to talk. According to a study by *Reader's Digest*, women speak an average of fifteen thousand words per day, and men are said to use only about three thousand. For some men, by the time they get home in the evening they have already depleted their quota for the day; however, a wife may just be getting warmed up. God has made us to complete one another, not to compete with one another.

The part of the brain where men solve problems is more in the back of their brain and it stores information there that helps us weigh out the decisions we are faced with. Men process facts. Ladies, you may be married to a guy who is not slow; he is just processing the information you have given him.

Humor is located in the center of the brain. When humor is activated it releases a lot of endorphins and other good chemicals of pleasure. Healing inflammation actually takes place in your body when you have a good laugh. The Bible talks about how sadness dries the bones, but a merry heart is like a medicine.

God created our soul/mind to be integrated with the other two parts of our body. We are a masterpiece of God's creation. He created as a three-part being. We are a spirit that is eternal, a soul that is intellectual and emotional, and a body that is affected greatly by the other two. According to Dr. Leaf, 75 percent of all illness is a direct result of our thoughts. The average person has somewhere around 30,000 thoughts per day. So we can see the need to be able to control and direct thoughts that can be healing to us or destructive to us.

AS YOU THINK IN YOUR HEART

God made us uniquely special. We need to see ourselves physically healed, emotionally healed, and spiritually healthy as God created us and made us to be. We were created in His image. The word *image* is from a Hebrew word not only meaning "shadow of" but also "imagination or thoughts"—we're literally in God's thoughts.

For I know the thoughts that I think toward you, says the Lord, thoughts of peace and not of evil, to give you a future and a hope (Jeremiah 29:11 NKJV).

His thoughts for us are not like our thoughts that randomly move through our mind. God's thoughts are creative. God's thoughts are communication to us. Our thoughts may be more like daydreaming and have no connection to anything. God doesn't have a brain like us; He is a Spirit, so thoughts from God are destiny. God's voice doesn't come through vocal chords; His thoughts are sent to us to show us His enormous love for us. Just consider for a moment that God has thoughts/plans for you and me. It is huge to think about how God is pinging our hearts continually with thoughts that heal us and lead us to our potential. The difficulty is hearing or understanding these thoughts because of all the other mixture of thoughts that are contrary to the thoughts He has for us. For instance, someone who has toxic thoughts about themselves of never measuring up to expectations and feelings of insecurity will find it difficult to receive the thoughts of God that are building them up. It's not that God is not speaking, but we have not developed a healthy thought life to hear Him. The mixture in our heads says, "It's too good to be true." Instead of capturing that wholesome thought from above, we let it slide through as just another random thought.

Here is a simple criterion to discern the origin of thoughts. Here it is; are you ready? *God is good and the devil is bad.* God says things to you that will heal and build you up. The devil wants you to be toxic with thoughts of hopelessness and suspicion. We can choose the thoughts that we allow to settle into our memory.

> *Many, O Lord my God, are Your wonderful works which You have done; and **Your thoughts toward us cannot be recounted to You in order**; if I would declare and speak of them, they are more than can be numbered* (Psalm 40:5 NKJV).

Capturing these thoughts from the Lord toward us is crucial in being healthy in all parts of our life. Thoughts that are detrimental to our well-being may come from previous years of built-up disappointment that has never found a resolution. When something arises that stings you, the mind will try to connect with something familiar in the past, and suddenly you are reliving the former pain. Many times in the Old Testament God would require Israel to tear down the "high places" of the pagan nations they conquered. The high places represented the places of idol worship.

Obviously, we don't have physical high places, but we have high places of the heart. A high place could be where we have made an inner vow such as "I will never get close to another person and be hurt." That inner vow becomes a high place of thoughts that need to come down and be replaced by the thoughts of the Lord. We can do so by meditating and repeating, "I will trust in the Lord and not lean on my own understanding." That inner vow may show a lack of trust and will resist the thoughts of God concerning future relationships. The toxic thought of that high place could keep you distant from others and interpreting that distance as rejection. In reality, it's an inner vow that started out as a thought and has built a structure to fortify that thought. God says, "I have thoughts toward you, not of calamity." If we have thoughts of calamity, they will always clash with the thoughts of God.

TOSS TOXIC THOUGHTS

A word fitly spoken is like apples of gold in settings of silver (Proverbs 25:11 NKJV).

Over the years of pastoral counseling I have met with individuals who couldn't articulate why they came for counseling. All they knew was they were hurting emotionally and it had handicapped them socially and in their marriage. With the help of the Holy Spirit, we would begin to discover thoughts that had originated outside of their mind from something spoken to them in a moment of anger. Though perhaps there was forgiveness, those words turned into thoughts that created Technicolor pictures. The more they replayed the tape of that moment, the more the thoughts would grow into speculation. Now, what was a momentary experience has grown into a mountain. This mountain has now become the lens through which they see everything.

Allan was one of those individuals with a mountain on his back for more than 30 years. When he was six and playing with a friend his age, a much older person entered the playroom and told Allan he was not welcome here ever again. The bully thought they were being territorial and was establishing their turf to rule. Allan did not say anything to anyone but went home cowed from the rejection. At this point I know it must sound fairly benign, but Allan transferred that experience into thoughts and set up a high place to protect himself. Allan didn't realize that experience would paralyze him socially for the next 30 years. It all began with the thought, *Something is wrong with me; most people would not want me coming to their events.*

We are all guilty of using words that demean and pull down and cause the opposite of what God desires. Hurtful words that were spoken to someone didn't just form at that moment. They began with thoughts. Jesus said in Luke 6:45 that the mouth speaks out of the abundance of the heart. The heart represents our soul or intellect. The words we speak are coming from the reservoir of our thoughts.

> *And since we have the same spirit of faith, according to what is written, "I believed and therefore I spoke," we also believe and therefore speak (2 Corinthians 4:13 NKJV).*

The connection to speech and thought is closer than perhaps we thought. The sarcasm of a young child is a learned experience through the input of thoughts received. The way he is talked to is the way he will respond in the future. What may appear as a fun joke or prank to a friend could create a thought path that is not so funny in the future. Have you ever been around someone nobody likes to be around? Usually within five minutes this type of person is saying something ugly about somebody or something; they tear someone down to make themselves look big. After a few minutes of listening to the negativity, you probably feel yucky, slimed, toxic. I actually feel like I need to take a bath. Why? Because God didn't give those thoughts or words, and when we absorb them into ourselves we feel worse for it.

Chapter 2

HOLY SPIRIT CLEANSING

The Holy Spirit wants to cleanse us. I want to share the biblical side of that truth and how we can free ourselves from unclean thoughts that interrupt our thinking. The Bible talks about meditation and how powerful it is. When concentrating and meditating on the Trinity, you are using your mind in the best possible way. When you meditate on something or someone less than worthy—when you roll it around in your mind, mull it over, talk about it, think about it, and speak it out—it becomes a stronghold.

> *"Be angry, and do not sin": do not let the sun go down on your wrath, nor give place to the devil* (Ephesians 4:26–27 NKJV).

This verse gives great insight to how the devil infiltrates our open gate of thought. In this case, Paul gives three points of instruction. The first is to be angry without sin. The word for "anger" is not the destructive level but one that means not to boil over. The word picture is a pot boiling on the stove; as long as it stays within the boundary of the pot it is useful, but when it boils over the top, then it's at a destructive and harmful level. Second, we are told not to let the sun go down on our wrath. The point being, don't go to sleep allowing a thought of wrath to germinate and be sown into your memory. Wrath is the idea of making a final judgment and assessing penalty to the situation. For instance, setting a mindset against someone as a final perception of them from now on. Third, Paul says we are not to give the devil any place. The Greek word for "place" here is *topos* meaning geographical ground or territory. The strategy of the devil is to set up a base or staging area for greater infiltration at a later day. If he can start by suggesting that someone doesn't like us and letting us think it is our discernment at work, then we have given ground. The devil is a squatter; he will take any land that we are willing to concede through agreement. Agreement to our enemy is simply not disagreeing or pushing back on that suggestive thought.

Consider a stronghold as a chair in your mind that you have crafted for the enemy to come and sit on. The devil quickly makes himself comfortable and starts telling you ungodly things about other people and about God. *Has God really said...? Maybe God doesn't love you as much as you think He does.* After all, he is the accuser of God's people. The longer you allow him to sit there and entertain his insinuations, the more he wants to sit there until ultimately he becomes a frequent visitor. When a thought has been given a place it is formed into our memory or storage bank. It then becomes part of our thinking process from which we make decisions.

I believe this is what happened to the young woman in Abu Dhabi, and I have yet to shake her loose from that mindset. Her wrong thinking came from small doubts that built a wall around her heart. The enemy loves to confirm how you feel when you are feeling down and out.

When you're having a bad day and feeling down and then something else happens that seems to confirm that nobody loves you, nobody cares whether you live or die, the enemy loves to sit in that chair and declare, *You're right! No one does care about you!* I had this happen to me and I heard, *"You're only as good as the last message you preached and what they can get from you."*

Janet was an older woman in her mid-eighties. She came to me almost paranoid. She had been living alone for a number of years and had no one to filter her thinking. It was easy to pick up that most of her life she saw life through the optics of fear. She had a fear of making mistakes, even in the simplest of tasks. Janet viewed her heavenly Father as only a faraway entity of the afterlife. Having come from an abusive alcoholic father, she survived by denying that she needed any help and believing that her life was perfect, when in actuality she did not have a true concept of love. Love to her was having things done for you, and the idea of love being unconditional was foreign. When trying to explain how perfect love casts out fear, she would deny she had any fear.

One day she called Diane and me insisting she needed to see us immediately. She kept saying, "I am going to be sued." When we asked the cause of the lawsuit she would only say, "I don't know." I asked if she had received any papers from an attorney as to the nature of the suit and she answered no.

After some questioning, we were able to backtrack enough to understand the entrance of her belief. She had been to the hairdresser she had been using for a number of years. At the conclusion of the appointment, she tipped the young man and then hugged him. She noticed his wife watching and the thought entered her mind that his young wife was jealous and was going to sue her. She had spent several days obsessing over the scene in the salon, and now it had become her reality. We were able to finally help her to see that fear was the basis of her thought patterns and until she could know the love of God, fear would rule her thoughts. She was able to replace thoughts of rejection with thoughts that brought healing to her soul.

When thoughts go unchallenged they begin to grow and form roots. If these roots are allowed to continue they produce bitter fruit. The fruit that comes from fear-based thoughts will form personality traits that will trap one in a cocoon of loneliness and suspicion, and soon life is one big conspiracy.

Here is a helpful test for thoughts to discern whether they are friend or foe. "Did God really say that? Is the thought of His nature?" If He didn't say it, then don't give it another second of deliberation. If it sounds like the enemy or the antithesis of God, then reject it! Once you understand and are able to discern good and evil thoughts that enter your mind, then you are on your way to being able to control the gate of your mind.

TRUTH VERSUS FACT

The best example of the contrast between truth and fact is the account of the twelve spies sent into the land of promise by Moses. Numbers 13 gives the report of what they saw. Ten of the spies said, "It's exactly like God has said, a land flowing with good things, except the Sons of Anak (giants) are there and they are too strong for us." Two of the spies, Joshua and Caleb, saw the same things but with a different takeaway, saying, "The giants are not a problem because God has promised us this land." Joshua and Caleb saw the facts, but their decision to move forward was based upon what God said, which is the standard of truth. I should add here that Joshua and Caleb were the only ones of that generation allowed to enter the land of Canaan.

Everyone has had to deal with toxic thoughts about another person. Sometimes we justify how we feel. It may even be a fact, but is it true? Truth is not information; truth is a person called the Spirit of Truth. Jesus said in John 16:13, "When He, the Spirit of Truth, comes, He will guide you into all the truth." Facts are the way things may appear and in all honesty may be correct. Truth is not how we view something, but how God views it. A fact is the way I might feel about something, but the ultimate source must be the Holy Spirit.

God created us and knows our frame and what is good for us, so He must be the one to help us sort our thoughts from His perspective. For instance, someone might feel justified in not forgiving another person. The fact is that the person they are angry with has unjustly hurt them. Their choice is to focus on the facts and rehearse them to everyone who comes by and find those who will commiserate with them or forgive, which implies they will stop assessing penalty by getting other people to hate the perpetrator too. Truth through God's eyes sees that the unforgiveness will eat like a cancer and do more damage to your body, soul, and spirit than the original wrong that was committed could do. Revenge will never fully satisfy the injustice, and it won't stop the thoughts of being a victim.

God's plan is to place all of the pain on the cross with Jesus and allow Him to bear all your sin to release to you forgiveness. The reality is if we won't forgive then all the sin we have accumulated is not forgiven. Jesus in essence says, "Put it on My account, not on the account of the person who wounded you." This helps to keep a pure thought life from getting polluted by the things that cross our path.

When He, the Spirit of Truth, is operating in our lives to break through a stronghold, then He can guide us into all truth. When truth is not operating within us, we can be deceived, misguided, or misdirected. Without the conscience of the Holy Spirit, the lie will appear to be our reality though it began as a fact and not truth. Bad decisions and poor life choices stem from a foundation of deceptive thoughts that frame one's perception.

GOD HAS THOUGHTS ABOUT YOU

How precious also are Your thoughts to me, O God! How vast is the sum of them! If I should count them, they would outnumber the sand. When I awake, I am still with You (Psalm 139:17–18).

We all struggle with our own thoughts. Trying to control our thinking can be frustrating at times, but let's take the focus off our thoughts for a moment and consider that *God our creator thinks about us.* This verse describes God's thoughts as more numerous than the sand. If we used sand as the metric to measure the number of thoughts God has for us it would be more than a billion thoughts per cubic foot of sand. Wow—that's more than we can imagine. Yet God's imagination has plans for us that we have not even considered. God's thoughts are blueprints and strategies for us. God doesn't think like we think, with a brain having random, disconnected thoughts. God's thoughts are creative and give life and direction. We were created in the image of God, in the thoughts He has toward us. We were created with the ability to receive His thoughts. His thoughts will always bring a sense of peace and euphoria. His thoughts toward us are filled with life-giving strength and purpose. Just the thought that He is the Lord who heals me jump-starts my body into healing mode, whereas an hour of listening to the medical theories of illness and their names can depress the immune system. Proverbs 23:7 is the proof text for this—as one thinks in his heart so is he. So why not begin to think what God the originator of your being thinks about you? An atheist would have to convince their brains the opposite of how God created them. Their non-belief in God actually works against the nature of how they were created.

YOUR BOOK OF DNA

Your eyes saw my substance, being yet unformed.
And in Your book they all were written, *the days fashioned for me, when as yet there were none of them* (Psalm 139:16 NKJV).

Have you ever considered that you have a book of potential written about you in heaven? I don't think it is a stretch of our imagination that God has seen us before we were formed and recorded in some heavenly fashion His thoughts for us to grow into. Our substance and DNA is recorded in a book. Whether we fulfill all that is written in our book is up to us. I don't want to miss out on anything that was written about my potential. This book of DNA is not so unusual when you think of the other books about us mentioned in the Bible. Revelation 20:12 says the "books were opened." We know there is the *Book of Life*; Psalm 87:6 says there is a registry of those *born in Zion,* a type for worshipers; Psalm 56:8 says, "Put my tears in Your bottle. Are they not in Your book?" Your book of DNA in heaven is filled with the thoughts of God about you. No matter what you think about yourself, God has thoughts filled with your future potential. Aborted children have their DNA recorded in heaven. The reason scientists want the stem cells from these babies is because of the DNA they possess. Science knows there is life in these babies' DNA, and it is life that God the Creator assigned to them. No matter how science defines these unborn babies, they have recorded DNA. They are more than just a mass of tissue; God says, "I have thoughts toward them and I have a record of their substance."

FEARFULLY MADE

I will praise You, for I am fearfully and wonderfully made; marvelous are Your works, and that my soul knows very well (Psalm 139:14 NKJV).

Mankind is the only creation that God breathed into. When God breathed into man he became a living being, also translated as a "speaking spirit." None of the animals have God's breath and therefore are not spirit beings. In one sense God gave man a part of Himself or a kind of spiritual DNA. He formed us to carry the ability to commune and fellowship with Him so we could receive His thoughts and promptings.

One other unique thing about us is that we were fearfully made. I know this could carry a number of meanings, none of which is less valid than another. Take this thought in its simplicity as, "You were made to be feared." I am not implying that someone should be afraid of you or to be able bully another person. God created you and I to carry His DNA, and the devil is afraid of us for that reason. Colossians 1:27 describes a born-again believer as one who carries *Christ's glory.* When Lucifer was cast out of heaven (Isaiah 14 and Ezekiel 28) he lost the glory of God. The throne room of heaven is filled with the brightness and light of God's glory. When the devil sees you as a born-again believer, he sees what he lost. The devil knows the power of God's glory and thus he is afraid of you. The devil, acting like the serpent in the Garden of Eden, attempts to inject the same thoughts into us as he did to Eve, creating doubt and fear. The devil knows that if you ever tap into the thoughts that God has for you then the revelation of God's glory will defeat the evil one and cast out his thoughts from you, the redeemed of the Lord. Jesus prayed in John 17:24 that we could behold His glory. That prayer is being answered today.

WHILE YOU ARE ASLEEP

I will bless the Lord who has counseled me; indeed,
my mind instructs me in the night (Psalm 16:7).

If you're a "techie" type of person you will enjoy this verse. While we're asleep, our spirit is downloading upgrades. Or, for my non-techie friends, God is communicating with our spirit while we are asleep. Our spirit is receiving something from our Maker, our Creator. If a toxic "virus" attacks, all of a sudden the Maker installs a virus shield upgrade to deal with it. So the Holy Spirit continually transforms and upgrades us into a higher level of sensitivity and knowing about Him, so we're not *degraded* but *upgraded. Anything that degrades you is not God.* God is all about upgrading from glory to glory, transforming us into His image or thoughts. This is why it is important to listen to the Holy Spirit. He will reveal alternative thoughts that counter the thoughts that attempt to pull you into emotionally spiraling down. Perhaps this is the reason some have a battle at night when it is time to sleep and commune with the Spirit. If you are one who struggles getting enough sleep, try praying like this, *"Jesus, You give Your beloved sleep; therefore I place my body, soul, and spirit into Your hands tonight. Let my dreams be directed by You and refresh my body for Your service."*

HOW TO SHRINK PROBLEMS

To deal with problems, you need to have higher thoughts. When you make the presence of God bigger, you overshadow the problems. Magnifying the Lord means making Him bigger than the problem. The problem will shrink when the solution is magnified. What we enlarge overshadows us. We just need to choose what we are going to enlarge. Who or what we magnify is who or what we worship. If the problem is magnified then we can't see the solution. "O magnify the Lord with me, and let us exalt His name together" (Psalm 34:3). Letting the thoughts of God increase to the point they drown out the thoughts of failure or disaster is the principle of magnification. Take an inventory of your thoughts or conversation and see what is magnified. Is the bulk of your thoughts or words negative, or are your words uplifting? Replace your thoughts or conversation with words that magnify the Lord. With enough practice you will find good things happening to you and better health. Proverbs 17:22 says, "A joyful heart is good medicine, but a broken spirit dries up the bones." You have already read about how thoughts greatly affect your outlook and health.

> *For as the rain and the snow come down from heaven, and do not return there without watering the earth and making it bear and sprout, and furnishing seed to the sower and bread to the eater;* ***so will My word be which goes forth from My mouth; it will not return to Me empty, without accomplishing what I desire, and without succeeding in the matter for which I sent it*** *(Isaiah 55:10–11).*

The *Word of God* is in synergy with the *thoughts of God*. We can develop a sense for the thoughts and impressions of God through knowing the Word of God. The verse above directly states that when God says something it is for the purpose of accomplishing something. Notice the analogy to rain and snow—they never return back in the same form as they came. Both water for the purpose of multiplying what they water. In the same way, God has given us His thoughts for the purpose of accomplishing His purpose. His purpose is the plans He has for you. Think of His thoughts being water upon your soul to sprout your potential. When there is agreement between you and His thoughts, multiplication and magnification takes place. When you agree with God's Word/thoughts, you bind on earth what is already bound in heaven and you loose on earth what has already been loosed in heaven. The word for "agreement" in the original text is *homologeo* meaning to say the same thing or to concede to. The contrast to agreement is to disagree or to say something different. The Holy Spirit may be attempting to get in agreement with you but you are saying the opposite than God's thoughts for you. For instance, if you are calling yourself stupid or dumb then you are in disagreement with God and the Holy Spirit cannot move on your behalf due to the synchronization of your thoughts.

Isaiah 55:8 says, "My thoughts are not your thoughts, neither are your ways My ways." We are not able to mix our thoughts with His and expect any change. He doesn't have to agree with our line of thinking, but we have to agree with His in order for miracles to take place. For example, someone could say, "I have been thinking about getting a divorce, and in thinking about all the rational reasons I have decided to move forward with it." His thoughts trump our thoughts because they are higher. It's not profitable to think everything that passes through your head is a God-created thought. The Bible says in Proverbs 3:5, "Trust in the Lord with all your heart and do not lean on your own understanding." The thoughts of God will renew and heal minds in order to establish His understanding. Decision making becomes easier when we have godly understanding.

> For **you will go out with joy and be led forth with peace;** the mountains and the hills will break forth into shouts of joy before you, and all the trees of the field will clap their hands. Instead of the thorn bush the cypress will come up (Isaiah 55:12–13).

The result of godly thought agreement is that joy breaks out, and instead of getting thorns we get real fruit.

In Jeremiah 29:11 God says, "For I know the thoughts that I think toward you, says the Lord, thoughts of peace and not of evil, to give you a future and a hope" (NKJV). My paraphrase of this favorite verse is: "I haven't been thinking bad things about you. I didn't send My Son to die so you'd have a worse time of it. The transformation in your inner self comes about so you can delight yourself in Me, the Lord, and I'll give you the desires of your heart. But if the thoughts of your mind are set upon evil desires, I can't answer that, because they are not in agreement with my plans for you." The word for "thoughts" in the above verse means to *imagine or fabricate and weave together*. God's plans start with giving us thoughts or a godly imagination that will work toward weaving a destiny. Thoughts create pictures, and pictures create destinies.

We can know if the thoughts we are meditating on come from God. His thoughts will always be of *peace* with *hope* and set a platform for your *future*. If you are not sensing peace you can know that it's not a God thought. We were created in the thoughts of God; therefore, we can say that our best future depends upon an intimate relationship with Him who created you. We *cannot* be thinking or saying, "God, give me what I'm asking for, and give to that guy who hurt me what he deserves because he needs to be taught a lesson." No. The thoughts of God are not mercy for you and judgment for everybody else. The mercy that you give out is the mercy that you will receive. Agreement with God is not just for you; you are also to be in agreement over how God feels about others. Part of learning how God thinks is to filter your thoughts through the mind of Christ.

We destroy toxicity in our minds when we refuse to have a double standard—one standard for us and another standard for others. Blessings and cursing cannot coexist and have a healthy thought life. It totally changes your whole perspective about a person or situation when you start thinking from the point of view of Jesus and the cross and the price He has paid for our sin. God has things on His mind for you, just like a parent says when his or her baby is born, "I've got plans for this baby to grow up and be successful." God has plans for us, and when we come into agreement with His plans our lives will be abundantly full.

JUDGING HEART THOUGHTS

For the weapons of our warfare are not of the flesh, but divinely powerful for the destruction of fortresses (2 Corinthians 10:4).

Paul describes the warfare or strategy of the spiritual realm that attacks our mind. The word for "fortresses" in this context is *noema,* which means "thoughts." Reading this verse with the translation, it says *our weapon is not of a natural kind but is of the power of the Spirit for the purpose of destroying thought structures.* We build forts with our thoughts. If you have ever known someone who just could not bend to ask for forgiveness or to receive forgiveness, chances are they have built a fortress that has blockaded their mind to any change of thought. The way one would build a physical fort is the same way one would build a spiritual fort—by placing one log on top of the other creating a wall or barrier. Most mental forts don't happen overnight. They are an accumulation of hurtful and resentful thoughts cemented together with bitterness. They were never challenged, so eventually they became a base of operation. Feelings and thoughts were now filtered and viewed through the portals of the fortress. It would also be a place of retreat that one could run into and hide when feelings were ruffled.

The Holy Spirit will begin to dismantle the security of the fort one misunderstood thought after another, until all the vain and bitter imaginations are torn down. Once those resistant mindsets are destroyed, the Master Builder starts building a habitation for His thoughts and plans. The strongest part of the fortress to tear down is *unforgiveness*. The last thing to be torn down many times is the first log of the mind fort.

> *We are destroying speculations and every lofty thing raised up against the knowledge of God, and we are taking every thought captive to the obedience of Christ* (2 Corinthians 10:5).

Paul calls these thoughts "speculations," meaning they are not truthful but twisted half-truths, which makes them untruthful. A thought that attempts to be raised higher than God, wants to sit on the throne of your heart and rule you. There are thoughts that can rule you unless you take them captive and bring them under your control. *Captive* literally means "at the point of the spear." You are to directly dominate that thought by using a weapon to cause it to come down. The weapon we use is the Sword of the Spirit, which is the Word of God—replacing a lofty thought with a ruling thought from the Holy Spirit.

We must destroy unfounded speculations—destroy any lofty thought elevating above God and the knowledge of God. So if my knowledge of God is that He will never forsake me, He keeps His covenant with me, and He shows me mercy, then I must not allow any other thought to influence my thoughts. Therefore, if a thought comes in that says *God has abandoned me*, I know that is not the truth—rather, it's a thought I must destroy.

Now here's the interesting part of this:

We are taking every thought captive to the obedi-
ence of Christ, and we are ready to punish all
disobedience, whenever your obedience is complete
(2 Corinthians 10:5–6).

Disobedience is punished through obedience. Disobedience is simply accepting thoughts or ideas that God did not
initiate. Someone may have passed on some juicy gossip others
said about you. Sure, there is the initial sting. If those delibera-
tions continue to linger they always grow beyond the original
words. We tend to add our assumptions to the mix and suddenly we have a picture that is eating away at the inside of us.
To *punish*, meaning to "send it away," we first acknowledge to
ourselves that the picture is not true and your heavenly Father
did not send you that garbage. Second, we set our hearts on
thoughts God has said about us, such as "You are my son or
daughter" and "I am well pleased with you." The punishment
to the thought is that it no longer has a place of prominence.
You refuse it a place at the table of discussion, and when it
doesn't get fed it dies for lack of repetition. When we repeat
something we are giving life and longevity to the issue.

VIRUS-FREE

I'll tell you, it's work to stay virus-free. It is work to build
up your spiritual immunity to where things don't come and
stick on you. We've trained our brains to be skeptical. We've
trained our brains to think something bad is right around the
corner. We build the fortress out of assumptions that have a
modicum of truth but overall are not real.

Ben was a pastor I had known for a number of years. We enjoyed good fellowship together every time we saw each other. I had ministered in his church many times. On one occasion, he asked me if I would dedicate the building they had just completed. After working out a few details of scheduling, I said I would be honored to speak at the dedication. The evening of the event Diane and I drove three hours to be there. Our schedule leading up to the service had been taxing to say the least. The service went long, as expected in these types of gatherings with all the usual pomp and circumstance that a dedication called for. I delivered my message of dedication and enjoyed the response from the audience, and I felt good about the evening.

After the meeting Ben asked us if we would wait for him in a side room until he had finished with his guests. We waited over 45 minutes without knowing what was happening anywhere else in the building. It was about 11:00 at night and we were feeling exhausted. Diane and I decided to head on to our hotel. After that, I would occasionally see Ben at other conferences and such with very little more than a, "Hi, how are you?" It did seem somewhat different from our past friendship. It was about four years later that I was speaking at a small pastor's luncheon and Ben was there. He asked before I spoke if he could speak with me afterward. When we talked, he began by asking for forgiveness; I was still in the dark as to why he needed to do that. He told me, "I made a judgment that you were not approving of the dedication service four years ago. I saw your face and you seemed disconnected, and then you didn't wait for me."

I offered my apologies as well and explained to him that I loved the meeting and perhaps my long day of weariness was showing and the reason we left was because it was just too late to stay any longer. We both realized that four years of wrong assumptions had robbed us of our friendship.

The message here is that we are not always right in how we read body language, and we never know what someone else is going through. The quicker we resolve suspicions before they can become strongholds, the healthier our minds will be.

Now here's the test. The psalmist says in Psalm 119:11, "Your word I have hidden in my heart, that I might not sin against You" (NKJV). I actually believe that to have thoughts is not a sin, but there are thoughts that continue to grow beyond the original entrance that cause us to become bitter, which is sinful—it has invaded and polluted our mind. I'm not just talking about pornographic, perverted thoughts. I'm talking about thoughts that oppose the nature of God.

Hebrews 12:15 tells us:

> See to it that no one comes short of the grace of God; that **no root of bitterness springing up causes trouble**, and by it many be defiled.

Bitterness starts with a seed that grows into a tree on which bitter fruit grows. "I want them to think like I think and I'm going to hammer them until they think like I think." Bitterness doesn't happen one day suddenly. It is a festering scenario that is replayed over and over until it's recited easily and with skill, not missing one detail. The sad thing about bitterness is that it doesn't just stop with one person but is like a vine climbing a wall—it grabs hold of the nearest person and covers them up with bitterness too. Sometimes we get annoyed at friends and family who won't buy into our diatribe and take our side. Bitterness is like misery—it wants company, in fact, the more the merrier. When we look back and see what it has stolen from us and how petty the issue really was, it makes us even more saddened.

THE MIND OF CHRIST

For who has known the mind of the Lord, that he will instruct Him? **But we have the mind of Christ** (1 Corinthians 2:16).

It does seem strange that we could possibly think like Christ thinks, but it's true—we have the potential of a renewed mind that is able to think the thoughts of Christ through the indwelling of the Holy Spirit. Jesus told us that when the Holy Spirit came He would take what was of Christ and give it to us. This tells me we can ask for the Holy Spirit to teach us to have the thought processes that Jesus had while in His earthly body. We know from Scripture that Jesus forgave people as He was hanging on the cross, while they were mocking Him. He forgave in the face of abuse and modeled the same mind for us. Stephen must have received the mind of Christ because we see him being stoned for his faith and forgiving those who were stoning him. Stephen looked into heaven and caught the gaze of Jesus standing on the right side of God. He chose to set his affections upon Jesus instead of setting his anger toward people who were misinformed.

I believe the Holy Spirit really wants to heal us in this area of allowing Him to cleanse our thoughts and the wounds those thoughts have caused. Our spirit is not the part that gets offended; it's our mind that picks up the offence, and it is our mind that can be renewed to the original manufacturer specifications—the *mind of Christ*.

Chapter 3

HIS POWER OF LOVE

We were created in the image of God. The word *image* here doesn't mean a picture of God. God is Spirit. He is not recognized the way we would recognize one another by outward facial features.

We have a dimension of God on the inside of us. Second Corinthians says, "You are our letter, written in our hearts, known and read by all men; being manifested that you are a letter of Christ, cared for by us, written not with ink but with the Spirit of the living God, not on tablets of stone but on *tablets of human hearts*" (2 Corinthians 3:2–3). The stamp of God's ownership is upon the inner being of all of us. Those who recognize that redemption call will invite Him in to be Lord of their life.

In my book, *The Power of Imagination*, I have written that we were created with God thinking of us and the imagination was a prophetic view of what we could become. God thought about us before we ever entered into our mothers' wombs.

This perspective gives us a big picture of how magnificent God is. We cannot reduce Him to a faraway person with a beard sitting on a big throne in heaven holding a big stick waiting for us to get out of line so He can whack us. His thoughts for us are for welfare and not for calamity. When we are able to let His imagination be in us then we can see our prophetic destiny.

OUR SHELTER

He who dwells in the shelter of the Most High will abide in the shadow of the Almighty. I will say to the Lord, "My refuge and my fortress, my God, in whom I trust!" (Psalm 91:1–2)

The word *shelter* means a place of protection. It doesn't necessarily mean a building. It's a position of dwelling. Some would call this shelter a type of the favor of the Lord. One word the New Testament uses is the term *abide*. John says, *"If you abide in Me, and My words abide in you*, ask whatever you wish, and it will be done for you"* (John 15:7). The word translated "abide" means "to pitch your tent," which is the idea to settle into and put down roots and live there, not just an occasional visit on Sunday. The favor to have prayer answered is incumbent upon where one dwells. Abiding calls for roots to be entwined around the thoughts of God so the requests we pray are really the desires that the Holy Spirit places inside of us. His desires become our desires; old desires of carnal thinking pass away. So my question still stands: Where do you live?

While in a prayer line, a lady asked me why people just dumped all their gossip on her. She seemed to be the person they called to pass on the garbage about someone else. I simply told her it was because that was where she emotionally lived; she was abiding in the dump. I told her to put up a no trespassing sign that says, "No dumping allowed." I advised her, "Next time they call and say, 'Have you heard the latest,' just tell them 'No, I have not, and I don't have any room for garbage.' I guarantee that will be the last time you will get a call like that. Soon the word will be out that you have moved from the dumping ground to the holy ground."

Psalm 91:1 says that we are to abide under the shadow of the Almighty. For many years I just accepted the idea of His shadow being like a cloud, similar to what covered the Hebrew nation in the desert after the exodus from Egypt. When I discovered that it was much more, the revelation of the shadow gave me a new understanding of how close our God wants to be to us. The Hebrew word for "shadow" is *tsalal*; part of the meaning is to vibrate like vocal chords would vibrate. It is similar to the word used in Genesis when the Holy Spirit brooded over the face of the deep. The word in Genesis is *rachaph*, again meaning to flutter or vibrate over. The idea is brooding over or inseminating.

Considering that overshadowing implies something being inseminated or fertilized and we were created through the thoughts of God, I believe we could conclude at some level that this shadow is God's thoughts over us. I get excited when I paraphrase Psalm 91:1–2 as, "I live and put down roots under the thoughts of God. I will say He is my shelter and He covers me with His thoughts of welfare and hope for a good future." I don't think it is a far stretch to believe we are under the overshadowing of God's thoughts, and through the Holy Spirit our hearts are being fertilized as good ground to receive the seed of His Word.

There was a similar experience while Jesus was on the Mount of Transfiguration with Peter, James, and John. "While he was saying this, a cloud formed and began to overshadow them; and they were afraid as they entered the cloud. Then a voice came out of the cloud, saying, 'This is My Son, My Chosen One; listen to Him!'" (Luke 9:34–35). We may not hear an audible voice daily, but I think we can have encounters knowing that He wants to communicate in our hearts with thoughts of His making.

When we understand the Lord's thoughts about us are so numerous we can't even count them, it makes the sarcastic, offensive remarks others might throw our way seem like just a wisp of smoke being blown away.

THE REAL YOU

When we acknowledge how powerful our thoughts can be, we open a whole new world of possibilities. As Dr. Leaf says, we can literally change our physical problems. Some people have high blood pressure because they have anger issues. Some people's eating habits cause health problems. Some people are under a lot of stress and develop ulcers and other digestive disorders. But if we begin to think like God thinks, then we can have what He created us to have—genes from our heavenly Father, not genes handed down from an angry parent or an angry society or a bunch of angry people around us. In Dr. Leaf's book, *Who Switched Off Your Brain*, she discusses how genes are turned on and off by either healthy thoughts or toxic thoughts. Toxic thoughts turn off certain genes that fight diseases. It is quite disturbing to think that we could be making ourselves sick simply by what we are thinking or allowing to enter our cognitive process.

When you recognize a toxic thought by its disturbing anxiety, stop and reroute your thinking with prayer, meditating on verses of Scripture that have to do with God's goodness and His power. Continue with the process of renewing your mind until you sense the heaviness lift. We can choose what we think. Sometimes it's a battle, but you will soon learn not to let it get a foothold and build a fortress.

First Corinthians was written by Paul. In chapter 2, he shares about a man caught up into the third heaven; most agree he was speaking of himself in the third person. He doesn't tell us everything he saw there, but he gives us insight that is different from all the other writers. Paul talks about spiritual encounters and revelation:

> *For to us God revealed them* [these things] *through the Spirit; for the Spirit searches all things, even the depths of God. For who among men **knows** the thoughts of a man except the spirit of the man which is in him? **Even so the thoughts of God no one knows except the Spirit of God*** (1 Corinthians 2:10–11).

The Holy Spirit knows the thoughts of God. He is called the Spirit of Truth. Truth is not information; truth is a Spirit or third person of the Trinity. We don't really even know ourselves, but our spirit knows us. The real you is your spirit. Your personality is you trying to express who you really are. This is where the disconnect comes in. Our soul or personality wants to be dominant. Have you ever said something and thought, *Where did that sarcasm or personal shot come from? I really didn't mean it like it came out.* The real you, or your spirit, knows the mind of Christ, but the part of us that expresses our personality takes the lead. When our mind is dominated and influenced by the culture around us, our spirit man is suppressed to silence. Without a renewed mind that is submitted to our spirit we will have conflict. Conflict is the clashing between two points of will.

Before the fall of Adam and Eve, God would communicate with them through His presence. When His presence was near they understood His thoughts without verbal language. Adam and Eve were dominant in their spirit to know the things of God. Adam was able to name all the animals and lived in the manifested presence of God; it was not difficult to know the thoughts and intents of God. When they both ate from the forbidden Tree of the Knowledge of Good and Evil their eyes were opened. That doesn't mean they were blind before, but it meant they saw things differently. They no longer saw with their spirit but now used natural senses. They both saw each other naked for the first time. Before, the glory was their covering; now, they saw through the natural and lost the lens of the supernatural. Everything flipped at that moment of rebellion. They became dominant in their soul (*psuche*, where we get the word *psyche* from), and their mind was now on top. Their spirit, that once was the lead receptor of God's presence, was now in conflict with their mind.

Remember, it was Paul who said, "For the mind set on the flesh is death, but the mind set on the Spirit is life and peace" (Romans 8:6). After the fall of man, the carnal mind came into conflict with the spirit of God. Romans 12:2 says, "Do not be conformed to this world, but be transformed by the renewing of your mind, so that you may prove what the will of God is, that which is good and acceptable and perfect." We can see why Paul, who had insight into the heavenly, said that transformation comes from having a renewed mind like Adam had before he chose knowledge over spirit. Jesus came as the second Adam (see 1 Corinthians 15:45) to restore you and me to the mind of Christ so we can receive the thoughts of God that will transform us into the fullness of Christ. The first Adam failed in his garden (Eden); the last Adam, Jesus, overcame in His garden (Gethsemane).

Our spirits are looking for the meat of God. Jesus said, "It is the Spirit who gives life; the flesh profits nothing; the words that I have spoken to you are spirit and are life (John 6:63). The things that God speaks to our spirit are foreign to the unrenewed mind. Psalm 42:7 says, "Deep calls to deep." The psalmist beautifully describes the call from our spirit unto the Spirit of God. The yearning of our deepest part—yearning to be in union with the manifest presence of God. We were created to commune with the God of the universe, our Creator.

The word *deep* or *depth* or *mystery* is the Greek word *bathos,* meaning that which isn't seen with the natural eye or senses. In Luke 5:4 it says, "When He [Jesus] had finished speaking, He said to Simon, 'Put out into the deep water and let down your nets for a catch.'" Peter, being an experienced fisherman, attempted to explain that it was not a good time to fish. They had been fishing all night and had not caught anything, but Peter said that at Jesus's word he would let down the nets. When they obeyed Jesus, they caught so much fish they called for their partners to bring another boat to handle all the fish. Peter had to choose between letting his mind or his spirit lead. His natural mind was thinking about fishing conditions.

THE BATTLE FOR HOLY GROUND

Olga was from Ukraine, fluent in both Russian and English and living in the United States. She desired for God to use her in the ministry of healing. She had seen much oppression from diseases and felt helpless to do anything about it. Every time she would pray for someone, her mind would take over and all she could think about was the disease and how powerful it was. She saw herself as small and the disease as a giant. She started reading from my book, *The Power of Imagination*. She learned that the battle against the disease was also a battle against her thinking. She read how Jesus said that if you look upon a woman to lust after her, you have committed your heart to adultery. She read further where I explained if the principle is that looking causes your heart to commit to the thing you are seeing, then it is also true that if you look intently at the goodness of God and His power and mercy, you have committed your heart to the power of God. This obviously is not staring at something with your eyes but the eyes of your heart. Olga soon started imagining what it would be like to see the blind healed. She started to dream about it in her sleep. Her dreams became more consistent with dramatic miracles of various kinds. She wrote to me to say, "I am no longer battling failure over praying for the sick because I already see them healed."

Our spirit already knows about the power of God. Cooperation with the mind is the issue. The fear of failure is a huge ruling factor when it comes to stretching our faith. The mind locks on to the path of experience. It resists due to past experiences. However, your spirit doesn't lean on past experiences but leans into the Holy Spirit for the now impression. Your spirit is looking for the green light while your mind has a foot on the brake.

In Ephesians 6:10–18, Paul is teaching the church concerning the battle of the mind. He uses the armor of a Roman soldier for the illustration to show we need armor in the spirit just like we would use in physical warfare. The armor is ordered the same way a Roman soldier would put it on. I am not going into the full armor, but I will extract a couple of connections to the battle of the mind. Paul wants us to first understand that the attack is not of human making. The devil likes it when we blame flesh and blood for our difficulty. He describes the enemy by rank. They are listed as principalities, which are spirits over regions; powers are designated to afflict and divide and conquer; and spiritual hosts have a larger level of authority over groupings of demons. The mistake is to focus attention on flesh and blood as the problem. The offensive weapon Paul mentions is the sword of the spirit, which is the Word of God. Notice the key connector in all of the equipment is the belt of truth. The belt of truth holds the sword of the spirit and is fastened to the breastplate of righteousness. As you can see, truth is the foundation for a healthy thought life.

David prayed in Psalm 51:6, "You desire truth in the innermost being, and in the hidden part You will make me know wisdom." David wrote this during his repentance for the sin with Bathsheba. David realized if he was going to get free of the damage he had brought upon himself and his family, he had to allow truth to penetrate the secrets of his heart. Then, after allowing truth to take hold, wisdom will come in the hidden part of the soul. John 8:32 says, "You will know the truth, and the truth will make you free." The only truth that makes us free is not just the truth we hear but the truth we apply.

Many people know the truth but fail to make application, and the result is the same cycle of defeat.

The last piece of armor I will mention from Ephesians 6 is found in verse 16. Paul emphasizes this piece. He says, "In addition to all, taking up the shield of faith with which you will be able to extinguish all the flaming arrows of the evil one." The word for "shield" in the Greek is *thoorah*. It literally means "in the shape of the door." So Paul is actually saying, "Above all else, take the doorway and keep it." The door is the entrance into the house. We have doors into the soul through our eyes, our ears, and through our mouths. He calls it the shield or door of faith. With our mouths we can declare the Word of God, and faith comes by hearing the Word. In order to have the thinking of Christ we must be in charge of what enters into our thinking.

CONTROLLING ANGRY THOUGHTS

Paul the apostle tells us that the shield of faith is needed to extinguish the fiery darts. *Fiery* is the word *poroo*, meaning to inflame with anger or a point of ignition. We all have had those moments when one moment everything in your world is happy and suddenly there is an ignition. It may have been a single word, and immediately you are engulfed in the flames of anger. The shield of faith works at the doorway best. The idea is to extinguish the opportunity for things to get beyond the front door into other rooms of the house. Isaiah describe this scenario:

> No one calls for justice, nor does any plead for truth. They trust in empty words and speak lies; they conceive evil and bring forth iniquity. **They**

> **hatch vipers' eggs** *and weave the spider's web; he*
> *who eats of their eggs dies, and from that which is*
> *crushed a viper breaks out* (Isaiah 59:4–5 NKJV).

The viper's eggs are thoughts that the devil wants to plant in our minds and allow them to incubate. At the time of the ignition of anger, they hatch into our thinking to convince us that what we are thinking is true. If we don't guard the doorway into our minds we can become a hatchery for some unwanted invaders.

In Genesis 4:3–5, Cain and Abel, sons of Adam and Eve, brought offerings to the Lord. God received Abel's offering and didn't receive Cain's offering. Perhaps one reason was that Cain did not bring the first of the produce, whereas Abel brought the first fruits. Cain became angry, and God asked him, "Why has your facial expression fallen?" God told him, "If you obey, you will be accepted; if not, sin is crouching at the door (shield) ready to take you, but you must master it" (see Genesis 4:6–7). Notice what God is telling Cain—you have an opportunity to get control over this anger while it is sitting at your door; if you don't, it will master you. Don't wait until it begins to affect your whole household and then they carry the same fiery dart. When the memory bank starts searching for other angry thoughts, it creates stress in the body. Cortisol, acid, and other detrimental chemicals start dumping into the body. Then adrenaline kicks in and says, "Don't stop now."

We can't give angry thoughts time to recruit chemical reinforcements that will egg us on to things we will regret later. Whatever we feed will continue to live and hang around like a stray animal. Demonic spirits are attracted to being fed. A spirit of fear injects thoughts of fear into your mind to feed off of you reacting to fear. The Bible says it's not what enters into a person that defiles the person; it's what comes out of them. So is it a sin to eat fried chicken? No, it's not a sin. Is it a sin to say something ugly or mean to someone? Yes, because what comes out of the mouth or doorway is either blessing or cursing. Jesus was teaching His disciples how to respond to the different environments they would encounter as they were sent out to minister the Gospel. He said if you go into a city and they will not receive you, shake off the dust from your feet as a testimony against them (see Luke 9:5). The dust represented more than just that city. Remember that man was formed from the dust of the earth. The serpent was cursed to slither on the ground and eat the dust of the earth. If they left a city and held on to the rejection and carried that dust around with them into the next town, the devil would feed off that dust/rejection and use it as a doorway to torment them. It becomes devil's food cake for demons. This is why it is important to keep painful thoughts shaken off of you so they won't attract like spirits who come with flaming arrows to shoot. Isaiah 26:3 says that God will keep us in perfect peace if we keep our minds on Him.

PRAYER FOR CLEANSING THOUGHTS

Heavenly Father, I am ready to bring my thoughts into conformity to Your will. I ask in the name of Jesus for the cleansing of thoughts that have set me back and brought delay and losses to my life. I choose to release forgiveness to all who were used to affect my peace and unity with the Holy Spirit. I let go of being a victim of betrayal, and I refuse to replay the old tapes in my mind. Wash away all resentment and condemnation that have brought shame to my family and me. I ask the Holy Spirit to bring back to my remembrance all that You have done for me. I pray for a renewed mind so that I receive Your thoughts to replace the ones I have had previously. Bless my mind to be clear without any unhealthy habits I have allowed to dominate my thinking. Let the words of my mouth and the meditation of my heart be acceptable in Your sight, Lord. I believe for a change of thinking in Jesus's name, amen.

Chapter 4

SPIRITUAL THOUGHTS

Understanding the processes of thoughts and thinking is not a psychological exercise, it is a biblical principle. We've already read Scriptures that confirm it. And we have already established the fact that God has no brain—He is Spirit, so His thoughts are spiritual.

Psalm 16:7 tells us that while we're asleep thoughts are being downloaded into us—God's thoughts, even subconsciously. Sometimes we wake up and we think we didn't dream. We really did dream, but we just don't remember because dreams are at a deeper, subconscious level. When God gives thoughts to us, they are imparted into our spirits. Our spirits already know everything they need to know. When we're born again, we're born into who He is; because God is Spirit, we have an eternal spirit living within us.

I delivered a series not too long ago titled "The Power to Change." In essence, it was about how a lot of people want change, they believe in change, they desire change, they make

New Year's resolutions to get rid of bad habits and bad things, but they're not really committed to change; they're committed to the *idea* of change. When we're just committed to the idea of something, nothing ever changes. Romans 12:2 is clear that transformation comes from having a renewed mind. Some Greek words for "renew" also translate to *awaken* and *detoxify*. A mind that has been dull and insensitive that is awakened to its creative purpose is said to be renewed. A mind that has been decluttered from worry and life drama is detoxified; this can also be termed a renewed mind. A mind that is awakened to who Christ is will have the beginning of a renewed mind. A toxin is a poison, and it's possible to be poisoned with thoughts that work against who we were created to be. Romans 8:1 says, "There is therefore now no condemnation to those who are in Christ Jesus, who do not walk according to the flesh, but according to the Spirit" (NKJV). Condemnation is a toxin or poison to the soul—words that defame or curse instead of build and bless our soul. Husbands and wives, we live in the kind of marriage we bless or the kind we curse. We create the environment we live in through blessing or cursing. Blessing is healing to our soul, which detoxifies us, and cursing sickens the soul by injecting toxic words into the soul.

THE CAUSE OF A CURSE

Proverbs 26:2 says, "Like a flitting sparrow, like a flying swallow, so a curse without cause shall not alight" (NKJV). It's a poetic way to describe a flying bird needing a nest to land. If there is no nest the sparrow cannot land. In much the same way, cursing lands on us. I am not referring to the four-letter words called cussing. A curse is a toxic, painful word hurled in an attempt to place us in a lower position from what God had imagined for us. This verse is very telling because it gives insight into the reason some find themselves cursed. A curse cannot alight on us without having a cause. The cause comes by us cursing (placing someone in a lower position than God said), which is the equivalent of building a nest or landing strip for someone to curse. Blessing is speaking to others in accordance with the position God says about them. Saying things to bully or intimidate is setting up the curser for cursing to enter them. Revelation 12:10 describes Satan as the accuser of the brethren. When a person has trained their thoughts to receive cursing or speak cursing, then we have agreed with the adversary, the devil.

> *He also loved cursing, so it came to him; and he did not delight in blessing, so it was far from him. But he clothed himself with cursing as with his garment, and it entered into his body like water and like oil into his bones* (Psalm 109:17–18).

This is a really strong word to those who feel empowered through cursing others. Take note that cursing doesn't just leave their mouths, but it returns to their body and into their bones. As we said in the beginning of this book, thoughts and words of the heart affect our health greatly. Instead of getting free from this toxin many will mask its effect with antidepressants and other biologics. Proverbs 15:30 says, "A good report makes the bones healthy" (NKJV). God not only created us but also has given instruction as to how to be free from disease through having right thinking.

By now we should be able to understand that God's thoughts over us protect us from radical thoughts of cursing.

To replace thoughts and words of cursing with His thoughts of blessing is healing to our mind and body.

WHICH TREE ARE YOU GROWING?

Dr. Leaf says a collection of thoughts creates a structure in the brain that looks like little trees. Every thought carries information and forms a perspective or an idea. Each thought is like a packet of energy with potential. The memory holds on to these toxic thoughts until they are cleansed. Adam and Eve were never charged not to eat from the Tree of Life. They were only forbidden to eat from the Tree of the Knowledge of Good and Evil. My point here is that the thoughts we accept into memory are an indication of which tree we are eating from. The tree we eat from forms other little tree-like structures in the brain that affect every part of our life. The Tree of Knowledge is representative of this present world philosophy that seems to toss out any absolutes. With a steady diet of this tree and the toxic psychology of this present age, it's no wonder disease is increasing and depression is the new norm. The Tree of Life is representative of the thoughts of God that continue to renew the mind and heal every part of society. One of these trees, or perhaps a mixture of the two, will form in our minds. The clearer the thought is, the closer to the Tree of Life.

DON'T BE TAKEN ADVANTAGE OF

But one whom you forgive anything, I forgive also; for indeed what I have forgiven, if I have forgiven anything, I did it for your sakes in the presence of Christ, so that no advantage would be taken of us

by Satan, for we are not ignorant of his schemes
(2 Corinthians 2:10–11).

The apostle Paul is revealing the tactics of the devil and his attempts to divert agreement with God to himself. Remember, in the Garden of Eden the devil introduced the suggestive thought that God was keeping the first family from experiencing more than what they had ever seen before. The devil wanted their eyes to open to see life through his perverted eyes. He knew that if they tasted of life with a different mindset, they would lose the glory of God and be removed from paradise. He knew this because that was what happened to him. Lucifer, a.k.a. the devil, was a covering cherub in the throne room in heaven. Lucifer was surrounded with glory until pride perverted his thinking and pride over his position of worship director entered in. Pride always causes a fall, and he was cast out of paradise and fell to a planet of darkness. Now he is known as the prince of darkness. His rule is over darkness, and he knows the power of the glory of God. He could not rule over Adam and Eve unless they were removed from glory as well. So now you understand why he puts thoughts into our thinking and creates moments of offence in order to remove us from the covering or shadow of God. While under the thoughts/shadow of God we find refuge, and evil cannot find us there. Paul is exhorting the church in Corinth not to be ignorant of how the devil works. *Ignorant* has two specific meanings. One is to be uninformed or misinformed. The second is subtler and comes from the root of *ignorant,* meaning "to ignore." Some people are just not taught about the demonic tactics we face, while others might know but they choose to ignore them. In the case of Adam and Eve, they knew what God had said and chose to ignore the command to not eat of the forbidden fruit.

Let's examine four devices or strategies the devil uses to disrupt our place in the refuge of God's glory. Though these are not the only four, these are from his basic playbook.

1. **Unforgiveness** is the cardinal rule to break fellowship with God. In the above verse, Paul is mentioning that forgiveness was imperative for him to continue to experience revelation from God. Evidently, there was a person who was causing damage to Paul's efforts, and he said, "For your sake (those whom he was teaching) I forgave so that Satan would not gain advantage over us." Paul understood that unforgiveness would allow the devil certain leverage over him and affect the ministry of the Gospel. Immediately after Jesus gave the Lord's Prayer in Matthew 6:10–13, He says, "For if you forgive others for their transgressions, your heavenly Father will also forgive you. But if you do not forgive others, then your Father will not forgive your transgressions" (Matthew 6:14–15). The devil knows that unforgiveness will bring separation from the covering of glory and he then has gained a foothold and won't let go until we reverse the course of unforgiveness.

2. **Temptation** is the number two on the list. Being tempted is not a sin; however, submitting and succumbing to it is. The sooner we learn what is happening in the beginning of the temptation, the easier it is to resist and change direction.

I should make the distinction here between temptation and testing. God does not tempt, but He may test. James 1:13–14 says, "Let no one say when he is tempted, 'I am being tempted by God'; for God cannot be tempted by evil, and He Himself does not tempt anyone. *But each one is tempted when he is carried away and enticed by his own lust."* He goes on to say that after lust has conceived it gives birth to sin, and when it is full grown it brings forth death. The devil appeals to a weak area where a desire has not been submitted to the Father. A test is different because it is for the purpose of graduation. God tests for strength to see if the house is ready to go to the next phase of building. In the case of Matthew 7:24–27, Jesus gave the parable of two houses and their contrast. One was built on the sand and the other on the rock. Both experienced the same torrents of wind and rain, but only one stood, and that was the one built on the rock, which is a type of Christ. The testing was for strength, not for temptation or lust. The devil would like to make you think that his temptation was God's little test. God is not looking for a reason to fail you but for faith to elevate you.

3. **Deception** is perhaps the most difficult to detect quickly. This tactic is disguised within the church or among our family members or possibly a friend. One reason the serpent was able to deceive Eve was the serpent was familiar to them. The devil didn't show up with horns and a pitchfork. He worked through a familiar instrument. It could have been a co-worker; the thoughts appeared to be rational, and he even quoted what God said, albeit twisted. After he had appealed to her thinking, she rationalized that it was *good for food*, it was *pleasant to the eyes* (lust), and it was *desirable to make one wise* (pride). All the hurdles had been jumped—just one thing left to do, and that was to act on it.

> *For I am jealous for you with a godly jealousy; for*
> *I betrothed you to one husband, so that to Christ I*
> *might present you as a pure virgin. But I am afraid*

that, as the serpent deceived Eve by his craftiness, your minds will be led astray from the simplicity and purity of devotion to Christ (2 Corinthians 11:2–3).

Paul sheds more light on deception with this verse. God is jealous for you, and He wants us to have a red-hot, fervent passion for Him. First of all, we need to get married to Jesus. Be married to Him. He'll guide into you all paths of righteousness for His name's sake. The word for "deceive" in the Greek (*planao*) means to cause to wander or roam. Deception leaves one without direction, searching aimlessly for the truth, because deception blinds hearts from the simple truth.

All thoughts move in two realms—truth or error. There's no middle ground. If it's not all truth, then it's all error. Rat poison is 98 percent grain and 2 percent arsenic. It's not the 98 percent grain that will kill you; it's that 2 percent poison that will kill you. Jesus said the Holy Spirit will guide us into all truth—not half-truths, not partial truth or mediocre truth. What we behold, we become.

The word *deception* means to wander away. Diane and I were in a store not too long ago, and I wandered over to another aisle to see something that caught my eye. I was deceived by all the sale prices that suckered me in. Next thing I knew, I had to call Diane on her cell phone to find her because I wandered off and lost my bearings. People have told me that the reason they go to bars and strip clubs is so they can witness to people. Now, there are people who actually have ministries and are called of God to do that, but one such person telling me that wasn't called. The Bible says in the last days what is evil will be called good, and what is good will be called evil.

Deception has a rational appeal in the beginning, but then after a while we have wandered off course. Deception usually doesn't happen overnight; instead, it's a gradual acceptance of the surroundings until they become familiar and normal. Suppose you were piloting a plane and you set your course, but you made a two-degree mistake in calculating your arrival. Two degrees doesn't sound like much, but when you figure the long distance, the two degrees would cause you to crash. In the beginning it may not feel like a big deal to try something that previously was off-limits to your boundaries. The Holy Spirit will bring a sense of uneasiness and conviction; however, if we continue to ignore the warning of the Spirit we will enter into full-blown deception.

4. **Accusation** is the device of the devil that is a more direct approach to remove us from a position of peace. The idea of accusation is to bring a charge against one's life or character. Satan still attempts to bring accusations about us to God. The charges are much like a prosecutor in a court. The devil is legalistic, and he wants to show why God should not answer our prayer or show mercy. Jesus stands in our defense like an attorney and pleads our case. The good news is, when we are guilty as accused Jesus can testify on our behalf by saying, "I have taken their penalty on Myself. My blood paid the price for their sin, and Father rules *not guilty.*" Daniel 7:22 says, "The Ancient of Days came and judgment was passed in favor of the saints of the Highest One, and the time arrived when the saints took possession of the kingdom." An accusation is an attempt to disturb us to become defensive and distracted from the pursuit of Christ.

And the great dragon was thrown down, the serpent of old who is called the devil and Satan, who deceives the whole world; he was thrown down to the earth, and his angels were thrown down with him. Then I heard a loud voice in heaven, saying, "Now the salvation, and the power, and the kingdom of our God and the authority of His Christ have come, **for the accuser of our brethren has been thrown down, he who accuses them before our God day and night.** *And they overcame him because of* **the blood of the Lamb and because of the word of their testimony,** *and they did not love their life even when faced with death. For this reason, rejoice, O heavens and you who dwell in them. Woe to the earth and the sea, because the devil has come down to you, having great wrath, knowing that he has only a short time"* (Revelation 12:9–12).

Not only will Satan accuse us before God, he will use others to accuse you. It may come in the form of gossip about you, things that are not true. The object of the attack is to have you turn aside and search out who said what to whom. It becomes a frustrating and confusing witch hunt. It is oppressive to your soul, and the offensive wounding continues to widen the gash in your heart. Remember, our wrestling is not with flesh and blood. The word *wrestle* in Greek means to vibrate, similar to the idea of *injecting thoughts.* Think of it like wrestling against thoughts of intimidation. So our wrestling is with thoughts of accusation from the devil, accusing you of not praying enough or not being faithful. He will accuse you of being a hypocrite— anything to get you to give up trying to serve God. The only way the devil can get a foothold is through the thoughts of your mind.

One other form of accusation comes from us. Through wrestling with thoughts of failure or insignificance, the devil likes to plant the idea that God is at the bottom of your problem. The devil will help you to blame God for all the unanswered prayers and disappointments you are feeling. The ultimate goal is for the devil to accuse God using you to be the accuser. The Bible says that in all of Job's attacks and afflictions with mounting bad news about his family, Job never blamed or charged God foolishly. The devil, with all his tactics he used on Job, never could shake Job's heart for God. Though we may not always understand why circumstances have turned against us, one thing is for sure—God is not our enemy. He sustains us through all seasons of life. We are to let praise be in our mouths at all times under all circumstances. This is the best resistance to the devil's tactics.

Chapter 5

THOUGHTS OF DISAPPOINTMENT

R ob was a pastor who began with great expectations for his new pastorate. Like most new pastors, he soon developed a missions strategy for his small church. He envisioned the impact it would have on the city. He often would attend special conferences and hear the wonderful success stories from other churches of their miracle growth. Rob would return home and quickly begin implementing the new programs that he had acquired while conferencing. In the beginning, Rob and the members of his church enjoyed the excitement of what was to come. After a while, the expectations that he had promised the fledgling church began to wane. He first blamed the devil for the halting growth they had experienced, and then it was the lack of faith from the other church leaders. When nothing else seemed to be working, Rob became sorely disappointed even to the point of looking for greener pastures that would receive his vision for church. He eventually realized he had taken on the thoughts and intents of others. He had unwittingly borrowed another church model and started building around another person's vision. Rob came to an important revelation: "God has plans for you." Rob had failed to set his heart and affections upon the Lord instead of a ministry.

Rob laid down all of the assumptions that God would do the same in his church as He did somewhere else. This time Rob waited until he knew he was receiving the thoughts and plans of the Lord. The plans were simpler and dependent upon the Lord, not on a business model. The church came alive and was blessed of the Lord because it was born out of the mind of Christ. Rob was able to get direction firsthand, not handed down from someone else.

Many people deal with similar issues in their thinking when it comes to expectations. The Hebrew word for expectation (*tikvah*) is an interesting definition—it means a cord of attachment. It would be akin to an umbilical cord or a rope. When we have expectations, we are tied or attached to something in the future. This attachment gives us a sense of hope and future. Everything is viewed at that time through the filter of those expectations. Like the umbilical cord, we are nourished by the thoughts of a better day. There is nothing wrong with having expectation, but when our expectation is based upon assumption it could set us up for disappointment. My definition of *disappointment* is "preconceived ideas or thoughts that were never God's thoughts." God doesn't disappoint. In fact, God appoints. He appoints times and seasons, but He doesn't disappoint. An assumption is a belief based on communication that never took place. It's giving us permission to accept a thought or an idea as if it was really communicated.

We move on assumption and when it falls flat, we are disappointed and ready to assign blame.

Let me give you a simple but personal example of assumption. When I was a young teenager, I heard my mother give my older brother permission to go to an event and stay out beyond the usual time to be home. I *assumed* because she was giving him permission, it would be okay for me to have the same word to go, and boy, did that not go over well. When my dad got involved, there was no assumption allowed. He said, "What was said to your brother is not your word. You should have come and gotten permission for yourself and not borrowed anyone else's permission."

I find this to be true with Simon Peter, who followed Jesus. Peter was an experienced fisherman and understood the culture and the times of the Jewish people. However:

He rebuked Peter and said, "Get behind Me, Satan; for you are not setting your mind on God's interests, but man's" (Mark 8:33).

Jesus had been teaching the disciples that the Son of Man would suffer many things and be rejected by the elders and chief priests and be killed, then after three days rise again. Peter quickly took Jesus aside and rebuked Him, and that's what brought Jesus's rebuke to Peter. Peter is not so different from all of us. Peter had expectations for Jesus; after all, he had given up his business of fishing to follow Jesus. Peter was expecting something out of the cost he paid to follow. When Jesus began to teach about dying, it totally crossed Peter's expectations. He was disappointed in Jesus because it didn't fit the picture Peter had in mind. Peter had the expectation that when Messiah came He would rid Jerusalem of the tyrannical occupation of the Romans. So you can see how Peter must have felt when he heard of Jesus being killed. Perhaps Peter had grand thoughts of being second in command with Jesus to rule Jerusalem. Peter was right that Jesus would rule—not just Jerusalem, but the entire world—but not right then.

In the next verse after Jesus's rebuke to Peter, Jesus taught, "If anyone wishes to come after Me, he must deny himself, and take up his cross and follow Me" (Mark 8:34). Jesus was making it clear that you cannot have your own agenda or expectations of what you would like to see. You must pick up your cross and follow, which was total surrender. The cross wasn't like today—just a symbol of burden bearing. They knew that it was the instrument of death. The message of the cross was clear, which was to remove all self-centered thought and take on His mind and follow His train of thought. Everything from then on was to be filtered through serving, no more "what's it for me."

FAITH-INSPIRED EXPECTATION

*For I know the thoughts that I think toward you, saith the Lord, thoughts of peace, and not of evil, to **give you an expected end*** (Jeremiah 29:11 KJV).

When expectation is based upon the Word of God it's no longer an assumption; it becomes a personal word direct to your heart. You will not be disappointed, though you may have to wait for His timing to see it all the way to the finish. Proverbs 13:12 says, "Hope deferred makes the heart sick, but *desire fulfilled* is a tree of life." When your expectation is fulfilled, it brings healing and great fulfillment. Expectation is the hope of something that lies ahead, which is close to having faith. The Bible says that without faith it is impossible to please God. The disappointment comes when expectation is not centered in true faith. Wishful thinking is not faith; daydreaming is not faith. Faith is tied to the Word of God, not a whimsical feeling. Hebrews 11:1 says, "Now *faith is the substance* of things hoped for, the evidence of things not seen" (NKJV). Expectation is tied to faith, so we need to understand faith.

Faith is not a mind over matter idea, but it is the reality that God will do what He said. For instance, the word *substance* (*hupostasis*) means "to stand under." Faith has covering to it. Remember in chapter two, Psalm 91 showed us we are to abide under the shadow of God's thoughts toward us. *Faith is standing under the thoughts of God.* So we could say that without the thoughts of God, expectation is not based on faith. Now look at verse three of this faith chapter:

> *By faith we understand that the worlds were* ***framed by the word of God,*** *so that the things which are seen were not made of things which are visible* (Hebrews 11:3 NKJV).

Faith frames our expectation with the Word of God. When expectation is birthed through the Word of God, then there is assurance of its fulfillment. Jesus taught us to pray "Thy kingdom come, Thy will be done in earth, as it is in heaven" (Matthew 6:10 KJV). Even our praying is affected by faith-led expectations; instead of praying with wishful hope, now we are praying the will of God. When you are praying prayers with faith that means you are standing under the thoughts of the Holy Spirit. "Which things we also speak, not in words taught by human wisdom, but in those taught by the Spirit, *combining spiritual thoughts with spiritual words*" (1 Corinthians 2:13). The Holy Spirit will bring to mind spiritual thoughts, which we can use to pray spiritual words. Now we can see that we don't have to be disappointed because we are not praying or relying on our thoughts to have faith. Some people try to work up faith as if it's an emotional courage. The Word of God already is of faith; we don't have to give faith to the Word, it is of faith. When we act upon the Word of faith the catalyst is activated to start things moving and growing to an expected end. The reason we hide the Word in our heart is so we will not sin and so that we will have faith. Romans 10:17 says, "So *faith comes from hearing,* and hearing by the Word of Christ." Take note that faith is developed through hearing. When we are listening to things of opposition that conflict with the Word then we become dull of hearing and thus faith is weak.

Genesis 6:5 says, "Then the Lord saw that the wicked-ness of man was great on the earth, and that every *intent of the thoughts* of his heart was only evil continually." God was ready to destroy the whole of humanity because their thoughts were continually on things of selfish gratification and every kind of perversion. Not only were they thinking this way, but their intents were on living that way. When thoughts that are of the base nature of man go without being cleansed, the intent takes over. Action begins with a thought, and when given time to grow it moves into the intent stage, ready to be acted upon. God found Noah, a man whose thoughts were different from those around him. God knew his thoughts and knew what was in his heart. Noah found favor in the eyes of God because he thought differently, which resulted in his living differently. Due to God's trust of Noah, God gave him a plan of salva-tion for his whole family. Romans 14:23 says, "Whatever is not from faith is sin." Note the connection—faith-based thinking keeps our thoughts in favor with God. We can be trusted to hear the plans of God when our thoughts are on things that produce faith. Isaiah 26:3 says, "You will keep him in perfect peace, *whose mind is stayed on You*, because he trusts in You" (NKJV). Expectations that are developed through faith settle our mind while we are waiting in hope for the fulfillment of those desires.

Chapter 6

PERFECT LOVE
CASTS OUT FEAR

First John 4:1 says, "Beloved, do not believe every spirit, but test the spirits, whether they are of God; because many false prophets have gone out into the world." It is interesting—John in his letter to the church was teaching us to be aware that not every prophecy is from God. Can we for a moment make application here from prophecy to the area of thoughts? So we could say, "Beloved, believe not every thought that enters your mind because there are many false thoughts that you might have; but test the thoughts, whether they are God thoughts or demonic thoughts or simply your thoughts from some past painful experience." So the question is, "How do I test a thought to see which category it falls into?"

The idea of testing implies that there is an intentional awareness of the thought you are testing. *Does that thought strengthen you in any way; does it add anything to your being to encourage happiness or any helpful instruction?* Compliments, blessings, and kind thoughts or comments made to us have that feel-good moment and we want to hang on to that injection. *If so, try thinking about it again and bringing it up in your memory, reminding yourself of that pleasure right before you go to sleep.* If a comment made you feel small or demeaned in any way for the purpose of intimidating you or making a comparison to shrink who you are, then immediately you must dump it in the garbage and not pick it up again. You must be intentional to not ruminate on it any longer. If you can't identify why you are feeling despondent, think back to any conversation or recent experience that may have brought about the smallness you feel. You may have not caught it immediately and its effects are still lingering. To be able to dump the toxic thought, say to yourself, out loud if needed, "This is not true and it is not who I am."

People who have a healthy self-esteem will guard against others injecting their anger and pain into their minds. Humility has nothing to do with feeling bad about yourself. Humility is not about comparison to others but instead building up everyone. *Humility is a character trait of strength.* The sin of comparison is destructive and it calls for others to be measured by the standard of the one doing the comparing. Those who practice this usually have a poor self-image and they look for something or someone who is worse off than they are to elevate their perceived status. The Holy Spirit in you will help to be the sentry of your gate. He will give you the sense about what to do with the thoughts you are thinking or others are trying to get you to think. He will guide you into what is true and what is an enemy to your soul. Listen for the prompting of the Holy Spirit to maintain a healthy thought life. When a thought or comment has been difficult to shake loose from your memory, begin to pray for cleansing and listen for the thoughts of the Lord to trump or override the enemy's thoughts. If you need more help, read the Song of Songs and get engrossed with the love language Solomon uses to describe God's feelings over us.

WHERE DO THEY FIT?

Love has been perfected among us in this: that we may have boldness in the day of judgment; because as He is, so are we in this world. There is no fear in love; but **perfect love casts out fear**, *because fear involves torment. But he who fears has not been made perfect in love* (1 John 4:17–18 NKJV).

I believe that all thoughts can be classified into two categories. They will either fit into the slot of love or fear. I know that sounds pretty simplistic, and there are benign thoughts that are neither good nor bad. However, for the sake of determining whether a thought should be admitted to our memory bank or put in the trash, consider all thoughts to be either toxic or healthy. John is using love in this context as the very nature of God. Love is not a sentiment or a feeling; it is the very nature that moved God to act on our behalf. God so loved that He gave His son. The love of God has been found to be lacking nothing; that is why it is said to be perfect. "Perfect" (*teleos*) means finished or completed—nothing needs to be added. The Bible says we are to be perfect even as our Father in heaven is perfect (see Matthew 5:48). God has thoughts for us that give us a hope and a future, so we can conclude that His thoughts toward us are perfect for us and for our benefit.

God's thoughts are meant to bring us into perfection to have the mind of Christ. Dr. Leaf said, "God has made us 95 percent perfect and left five percent for us to choose." We are in perfect peace when we are thinking of His perfect thoughts. We have a free will to do what we choose with the other five percent. We are constantly making choices and decisions based upon our thoughts. Thoughts that are born by the Spirit of God will fall into the category of love.

The other category of thought is fear. John tells us that if we receive thoughts of fear then we have made a choice to reject the thoughts of love. Fear is torment-based thinking. Fear has its origins with the devil. Even the thought he introduced to Eve in the Garden of Eden was fear-based. The serpent suggested to them, "If you don't eat of this Tree of the Knowledge of Good and Evil you will miss out on all the possibilities and awareness that God is trying to deprive you of." Here comes the battle between love and fear. John says in the above verse that love casts out fear. The word for "cast out" is a violent act of strength much like Jesus entering the Temple and turning over the tables of the money changers and casting them out declaring the Temple was His Father's house. Faith doesn't cast out fear—only love trumps fear. We are to cast out fear by refusing it a place or platform to continue to speak. Ephesians 4:26–27 says, "'Be angry, and do not sin': do not let the sun go down on your wrath, nor give place [ground or opportunity] to the devil" (NKJV). The reference is to not allow the devil any ground to stand on to inject thoughts of fear. Fear can entail a number of things that cause confusion and doubt about your future identity.

When love is perfect in us, the contrast between love and fear is obvious. Love leads and fear always attempts to push. Second Timothy 1:7 says, "God has not given us a spirit of fear, but of power and of love and of a sound mind" (NKJV). The power of love affects every part of our being, including our health. We must understand that God has given us power over the thoughts of our mind. He made us to have a sound and stable mind; otherwise, it would not be possible to have the mind of Christ.

Love releases chemicals in the brain that are similar to the effects of drug addiction. Dr. Lucy Brown at Albert Einstein College of Medicine in New York did a study of couples who claimed to be in love for an average of 21 years. MRI scans were done of ten women and seven men. The scans revealed that the part of the brain that is dubbed the "pleasure center" showed strong activity, which is essential to the brain for good health. Some studies show that when love is a factor, 12 different parts of the brain become activated. We were made for love, and every one of us craves love. God has hardwired us to function better and more efficiently under conditions of love as opposed to those of fear. Having right thinking is more responsible for good marriages than previously considered. How we think about our spouse greatly affects how we interact with them. Suspicion begins with a thought introduced from the fear category, and if allowed to linger it becomes an attitude and eventually results in action. In my book *The Power of Blessing*, I teach how to change a caustic relationship around through learning how to speak blessing. We have the spouse we bless or we have the spouse we have cursed.

The devil knows that we long for love, so he puts out a pseudo form that isn't God's love at all but rather a perversion of love. Pornography has become the seventh-largest industry in the U.S. Ambient pornography surrounds us now more than ever, from advertising on television to the shopping malls. Dr.

William Struthers of Wheaton College, a psychologist with a background in neuroscience, discusses this in his book, *Wired for Intimacy: How Pornography Has Hijacked the Male Brain.* He describes viewing porn as a hypnotic state with a poly drug-like addiction. He says the images that create thoughts continue to linger for long periods. Like other drug addictions, pornography addiction calls for more of the drug, demanding stronger dosages each episode. With this hypnotic state of mind, the user rarely is aware of the amount of time that has passed while viewing porn. After the viewing, shame begins to set in for those who are convicted by the Holy Spirit. With shame comes the guilt, and the devil piles it on with thoughts like, "You are now a hypocrite, so you might as well give up trying to live a Christian life."

First Peter 1:13 says, "Therefore *gird up the loins of your mind,* be sober, and rest your hope fully upon the grace that is to be brought to you at the revelation of Jesus Christ" (NKJV). This verse tells us that we can take control of our mind. The term *girding up loins* is referring to doing battle. The loins represent our strength and mind relating to our thoughts and mental attitude. Protect your mind at all costs. As one thinks, so they become. Pornography is not only a hearing issue but includes all of the senses of the body. Most pornography is done in secrecy and alone. The devil didn't approach Adam and Eve together; instead, he went after Eve alone. Proverbs 28:13 says, "He who conceals his transgressions will not prosper, but he who confesses and forsakes them will find compassion." The devil operates in the dark and wants to make you think you are all alone in this battle. When it is brought to light, the roaches of pornography scatter. I encourage any who are battling not only the addiction, but also this hypnotic spirit that drives you to guilt and shame—you don't have to battle alone. There is more help today for this addiction than at any other time. It is prevalent in the church and out of the church. You must find freedom before it destroys your home and family; it is not a benign little secret sin, it is controlling every part of your life and every waking moment of the day. There is no moderation with this sin; the longer it goes on the stronger it is and the more it will take from you.

In 1 John 4:18, John describes fear as torment. Love protects and fear leaves us vulnerable. Philippians 1:28 says to be "not in any way terrified by your adversaries, which is to them a proof of perdition, but to you of salvation, and that from God" (NKJV). Fear is a sign to the devil that you are weak and vulnerable, ready to be taken down. *Perdition* simply means to fall away or falling away from the safe place of love. Remember, the two positions thoughts come from are love and fear. This verse reminds us that when we are living out of the fear category we are stepping backward or falling away from love. Love casts out fear and fear sucks us into its vortex.

Perdition is like the sport boxing. The boxer cannot throw an effective punch if he is leaning back on his heels. The strength comes through leaning forward. The one moving forward is taking the ground, not giving it up. First Peter 5:8 says, "Be sober, be vigilant; because your adversary the devil walks about like a roaring lion, *seeking whom he may devour*" (NKJV). Fear is the pool from which the devil likes us to drink our thoughts. He looks for those who are hanging around the edges with one foot in and one foot out. Being a double-minded person is not only a vulnerable position but is also a miserable one to be in. If we truly love Him, the Bible says the epitome of love is that you would lay down your life for another. Marriage is the most unselfish thing two people will ever commit to. We demonstrate true love by laying down our lives, our excuses, and our selfish desires. Grace abounds in love. Marriage is either a contract or a covenant. There is power in covenant because covenant implies that a death has occurred. There would have been no New Covenant without Jesus laying down His life for us. A contract is about protecting the one making the contract. It limits the liability without anyone laying down their life for the one they love. The power of the Covenant of Christ will cut through ties of fear and bind you to His mind.

FREEDOM FROM STRESS

Stress is not due to an event but is a reaction to that event. For example, a person notices a flat tire on their car; they can stress about it, thinking the worst. Another person might simply make a call and wait for help, not giving it any more thought than an inconvenience. Both people experienced the same scenario, but their reaction to that event was the difference between stress and rest. Stress is due to a person's perceptions and experiences and memories of how problems have affected them in the past. Stress can be a learned habit while growing up, watching parents and how they address issues that arise from life. Dramatization is not a personality trait but a learned response to circumstances we face. Fear can cause stress because fear projects the idea of catastrophe although nothing has happened. *Fear causes one to predict the worst, thereby causing stress as a response to an event yet to take place.* Sustained stress will lead to distress. Distress can cause physical complications such as headaches, digestion upset, elevated blood pressure, sleeping disorders, as well as exacerbating existing health problems. Because a large percent of health issues are related to thoughts of the mind, we would do well to know how to de-stress ourselves.

One of the factors that would enable stress to explode quickly is trust. The trust factor has a lot to do with how someone would perceive a situation as rest or stress. One who views it from a position of rest, takes it in stride and is able to think through the process without stress. I am not referring to a tragic event that would cause stress to any of us. But the average daily dose of life should not be stressful. Proverbs 3:5 says, *"Trust in the Lord* with all your heart and do not lean on your own understanding." The point is when our understanding of trust is not secured in loving relationships, we often feel alone and have nowhere to turn for help. The feeling of being alone can come even when you are surrounded by family. Loneliness is a trust issue. If you can't trust God to answer in time of need, then you feel all alone and your perception of the problem brings stress. Granted, there are some home or work environments that are just plain stressful and you might not be able to change what is happening outside of you, but you can take charge of what is happening inside of you.

The apostle Paul advises that we should deal with anxiety with prayer and thanksgiving so that "the peace of God, which surpasses all comprehension, will guard your hearts and your minds in Christ Jesus" (Philippians 4:7). There are two ingredients to dealing with stress; first is to pray, not just asking for stuff but communicating with God and presenting your heartfelt needs. Second, we are to find things to give thanks for. There is something about giving thanks that seems to calm stormy waters. I remember being invited to help a church walk through some difficult times due to leadership failures. I knew they wanted me to give a prophetic solution as soon as I entered the room. The tension was so thick you could tangibly feel it in the air. I asked the Holy Spirit to give me understanding of the situation and what steps needed to be taken before I arrived. The meeting began and the anxiety of others was painfully obvious and they wanted to clue me in on the latest. I gently interrupted and began by giving thanks for all the years that were fruitful and for all the people who remained faithful and so on. The more I could point to what was right and get them to think on those things, the more the peace of God seemed to surpass the obstacles. I said, "Now we are free to make good decisions."

I enjoy reading the story of Queen Esther—how God used her to save her own people from an evil plot. She was prepared by her uncle Mordecai to go before the king. Mordecai is a type of the Holy Spirit. She was instructed what to say and to remember that it was not a time to be thinking about herself. It must have been stressful because the protocol was for her to only enter the court when summoned by the king or else she could be executed. Esther came to the point of saying, "If I perish, then I perish." She had trust in her uncle and knew that God was on her side, and she was able to gain the favor of the king to turn the tables of the plot back on the enemy. Trust gives you the courage to face difficult challenges that normally would cause panic and distress.

PARTNERING WITH THE HOLY SPIRIT

After the resurrection of Jesus, He was gathered with His disciples and said, "As the Father has sent Me, I also send you," and then He breathed on them and said "Receive the Holy Spirit" (John 20:21–22). Jesus wanted them to continue the ministry that He had started on earth. He wasn't expecting them to carry on His ministry without His power to accomplish the same things they had seen Him do. He was enlisting them as partners in His ministry. The first time we saw God breathing upon or into man was at creation. They became a *living being* (translated "speaking spirit"). That breath of God gave a part of Him to man to make him perfect. Now Jesus was once again introducing the Spirit into these men He chose. They received the Holy Spirit, but in Acts 2:4 they were endued with the gift of the Holy Spirit with power. It was now evident not only to those whom He breathed upon but to many others—a visible sign the Holy Spirit had come upon them. The crowd outside that upper room heard them speaking in tongues they obviously had never learned. The world was never to be the same from that time on. Jesus said when the Holy Spirit came He would instruct us in everything. He was now called the Spirit of Truth.

This partnership still exists today, and He offers us the opportunity to receive the Holy Spirit. Being in partnership with the Holy Spirit allows us to know the mind of the Father according to Romans 8:27. With the baptism of the Holy Spirit, we are more sensitive to know the thoughts that He has for us. The Holy Spirit will guide us into the destiny the Father has imagined for us before we were ever conceived. The next verse is familiar to most of us. "And we know that God causes all things to work together for good to those who love God, to those who are *called according to His purpose*" (Romans 8:28). Notice the condition for things working together for our good is based upon being called to His purpose. He is not talking about becoming a preacher but being a partner with Him. He will worship through us (see John 4:23); He will pray through us (see Romans 8:26); He'll be fruitful through you (see John 15:8); and He'll restore what the enemy has stolen (see John 10:10). Do you see yourself as a valued partner? When you know you are not alone, it takes some of the stress out as you lean upon the Holy Spirit to guide you through times of difficulty. David said, "Even though I walk through the valley of the shadow of death, I fear no evil, for You are with me; Your rod and Your staff, they comfort me" (Psalm 23:4). We have a partner in the Holy Spirit who is faithful to perform all He has promised.

Chapter 7

WHICH SIDE ARE YOU ON?

So how do we get rid of toxic thoughts? It has been said by different experts that to break a bad habit or change behavior it takes 21 days. I will admit I am not an expert, but I do know by experience and the Word of God that we can change what needs to be changed and we can cleanse what needs to be cleansed through obedience to His Word. One can't cleanse something that they can't admit to. If it is not confessed as sin, change doesn't happen. Second, ask the Holy Spirit to fill you with the thoughts of *righteousness, peace, and joy* according to Romans 14:17. The next step is to see yourself as a new creation that is being newly formed with new thoughts from your Father in heaven. Allow me to give you a graphic to picture the thought of a new creation. Jesus gave a parable that is a good fit here and it goes like this:

> *No one tears a piece of cloth from a new garment*
> *and puts it on an old garment; otherwise he will*

both tear the new, and the piece from **the new will not match the old** (Luke 5:36).

Begin to see yourself as a shiny new model car with that new smell and no scratches. You are protective of who is going to ride with you, and you don't want them to put their feet on the new leather interior. The Lord wants you to be protective of this new model of you, and it's okay to be selective of who is going to walk out life with you and who affects your new environment. In the next part of this parable, Jesus says that no one puts new wine into old wineskins or else the new wine will burst the wineskin and be spilled and the wineskins will be ruined. Those to whom Jesus was speaking understood His point exactly. Their culture knew freshly squeezed grapes would ferment and expand, and an old wineskin that had been stretched to its capacity could not handle the new change of expansion.

We could make an application here to our thinking. Change is not always easy and it has to be intentional. Preparing the wineskin, or our mind, is crucial. Every day for 21 days, start being aware of what you are dwelling on for more than five seconds. Consider if what you are thinking is going to take you back to a point of hurt or a point of healing. The old wineskin is the former way we used to think and view our situations. If thinking a particular thought arouses a feeling of anger or sadness, just know that is not the path of thinking you need to stay on. The new wineskin is fresh and refurbished; it is ready to learn new ways of thinking and responding. It is expandable to be taught new actions. Have a few thoughts written down that you can immediately go to and read and meditate on. They may include a Scripture or a testimony that brings you into stirred faith. The replacement therapy of thinking blessed thoughts instead of cursed thoughts consistently will retrain your thinking.

Paul gives three points of similar instruction in Philippians 4:6–9. He begins by saying not to be anxious for anything, but through *prayer, supplication* (specific prayer), and *thanksgiving* let your requests or your heart be known to God. He is saying instead of letting anxiety build up, talk to God, and be sure to include a thankful heart in the prayer. The second point is to allow the peace of God to guard your heart and mind through Christ Jesus. He is emphasizing that the heart and mind must be guarded. The sentry to guard the gates of your mind is peace. If you are in an environment or situation where peace is being taken from you, guard your mind by removing yourself if possible so the old thoughts don't try to take over. Third and most importantly, Paul gives the measure of discernment for thoughts. In verse 8 he says, "Whatever is true, whatever is honorable, whatever is right, whatever is pure, whatever is lovely, whatever is of good repute, if there is any excellence [value] and if anything worthy of praise [deserving of mention], *dwell on these.*" We learned earlier in this book that toxic thoughts could lead to suppression of the immune system, but replacing toxic thoughts with blessed thoughts could jumpstart our immune system. Whatever lives must be fed. If the new wineskin is going to be healthy, it must be fed with new, healthy thinking. The reason it's hard to break old habits is because we feed into the old wineskin. I was asked one time in casual conversation, "Why do all the stray dogs seem to find my house?" The answer is simple—you are giving them table scraps at the back door. What has dominion must be fed. With this 21-day reset, the object is to starve the old negative thought pattern and feed the new and improved mind of Christ.

The prophet Daniel was taken captive when he was a young man. The Bible describes him as one who possessed an excellent spirit. To paraphrase this statement, Daniel's heart and thinking excelled and stood out from the culture he was captive in. He didn't allow the pagan worship to influence him to worship their gods or to take part in their moral depravity. There was something inside Daniel that enabled him to live in a place that was in such an extreme contrast with what was in his heart. Daniel lived from the inside out. What was happening on the inside of his being began to influence others around him. It takes a strong and dedicated heart to be the thermostat of your surroundings. One day Daniel read from Jeremiah's writings. The 70 years that had been assessed to Israel for their disobedience had come to an end. He fasted and prayed to find the answer to their release and what was to happen to his people in the days ahead. At the end of 21 days, he received help from the angel Michael. The angel said, "I heard you on day one but I have been battling the powers of darkness over Persia that kept me from coming earlier."

Breakthrough may not come when we would like, but the consistency in the 21-day period will change the way things have always worked against us, to things working on our behalf. Don't give up until you have seen the change in your thinking.

RIGHT BRAIN/LEFT BRAIN THINKING

"When you give to the poor, do not let your left hand know what your right hand is doing" (Matthew 6:3). Obviously, here Jesus is speaking about being generous when giving to those in need. The interesting part of this verse is the word *hand*. In the original translation, the word *hand* was not in the text. The original would have read, "Don't let your left know what your right is doing." The message of generosity was "Don't let one side talk you out of giving." We know the brain is divided up with a right side and a left side. We all use both sides of our brain; however, there are some areas of dominance that lean more left or right. One study shows the left side of our brain is more *logical and analytical. This side does mathematical calculations and is much more linear in thinking.* In contrast, the right side is more dominant in *areas of art, music, and imagery. The right is known for intuition and romantic feelings and is more sensitive to spiritual thought.* It appears that our sensitivity to faith and spiritual thinking would come from the right sphere. Notice the verse implying, *don't let the left side that is logical and linear in thought keep the right side that is sensitive to faith and spiritual intuitiveness from giving.*

Most of us could identify a friend who is more pronounced as an analytical person or one who is sensitive to music, etc. The way we think affects how we respond to various scenarios that happen in life. We see through the filter or side of brain that we are most dominant in. Look at the other mentions in Scripture concerning left and right. Jesus said, "He will put the sheep on His right, and the goats on the left" (Matt. 25:33). We also know that Jesus is on the right hand/side of the Father in heaven. I believe there is a message here that He wants us to develop right-thinking and grow in sensitivity and romance with Him. I am glad we don't check the left side of our brain at the door. We would not have any sense of rationality or decision-making skills. On the other hand, it would be fairly dull to only view God through the lens of our analytical thinking.

To be touched with a deep love for God is to be valued. Can we say, then, don't let the analytical side hinder you from experiencing the spiritual depth of knowing God intimately. We all have the capacity to have thoughts like His if we don't let the left side be in conflict with the right.

In Romans 7 we are given understanding of the conflict between the mind of Christ and the mind of our fallen nature.

> *For I joyfully concur with the law of God in the inner man, but I see a different law in the members of my body, waging war against the law of my mind and making me a prisoner of the law of sin which is in my members. Wretched man that I am! Who will set me free from the body of this death? Thanks be to God through Jesus Christ our Lord! So then, on the one hand I myself with my mind am serving the law of God, but on the other, with my flesh the law of sin* (Romans 7:22–25).

This body of sin, this working against me—the conflict between these two natures is the external versus the internal. Paul states that there is part of him that really desires to please God and be immersed into the mind of the Spirit and there is a part of him that leans toward the law of sin and death.

WINNING THE WAR

> *Therefore there is now no condemnation for those who are in Christ Jesus. For the law of the Spirit of life in Christ Jesus has set you free from the law of sin and of death. For the mind set on the flesh*

is death, but the mind set on the Spirit is life and peace (Romans 8:1–2,6).

Winning the war of the mind begins with deciding which side you are going to give yourself to. The legalism of trying to do all the right things (logical left brain thinking) without feeling any motivation of love is laboring under legalistic thinking. The law of the Spirit (right brain thinking) is moved by what Jesus has already done for me, not what I have to do for Him. He took all the sin and gave me freedom from having to use my cognitive thinking skills to figure out how to please Him. Just know that He wants to get personal and speak about everything; He wants us to be so open with Him that nothing is off the table of conversation. He already knows our weaknesses and still accepts us. The law was about getting good enough to come to Him. The law of the Spirit says, "Come to Me, all who are weary and heavy-laden, and I will give you rest. Take My yoke upon you and learn from Me, for I am gentle and humble in heart, and you will find rest for your souls" (Matthew 11:28–29). The old yoke was about never finding any rest.

Today, just turn over all the heavy thoughts and weights of trying figure out life to Him, and be renewed in the spirit of your mind. Do not pick up again the thoughts of past regrets and rejection, but let Him clothe you with fresh garments of praise. He will wash away cursed thinking and give you blessed thinking.

HIS WORDS ARE SPIRIT AND LIFE

Jesus says in John 6:63, "The words that I have spoken to you are spirit and are life." All spoken words first come from thoughts. When we realize that every thought has the potential to become something creative and every word is like seed being sown toward that creation, it makes me want to think and speak with purpose. The Internet began as a thought that went into an idea and someone acted upon that thought, and now today we are communicating around the world at the speed of satellite. Thoughts and words that build up others and heal their broken hearts are spiritual, so I want to consider carefully what I am going to give my mind to. Ask yourself, *Is that thought helping or hurting me? Is it suppressing my immune system or is it building it up?* We are what we think in our heart, and we can train our minds to choose right thinking.

Part II

CHANGE YOUR THINKING, CHANGE YOUR WORLD

Chapter 8

THINKING LIKE A SON

By now we should be able to see that changing our thoughts can change our world as we know it. For many people, their perception becomes the reality they live in. If their perception is a narrow view of themselves and the world around them, then their reality and potential of success is narrowed as well. We have attempted in this section to unveil the real you God created. The "real you" may be hidden underneath heartache and disappointments, but the "real you" our Creator imagined is still there in dormancy waiting for an awakening. I have seen this awakening happen many times, and I believe if you are serious about practicing the principles discussed in this book, you will witness your God-given DNA appearing. You will be one of those who have discovered a fresh identity and empowerment.

First John 3:1 begins with, "Behold what manner of love the Father has bestowed upon us, that we should be called children of God!" (NKJV). Right away God wanted to establish a new identity with us. Under the Old Covenant they were not allowed to come close in a personal relationship. They could only perform rituals and duties to get any favor at all. In the New Covenant Jesus bridged the gap that the fall of Adam had created. God gave a Son to reveal the new relationship He wanted to have with mankind. He didn't send an angel or another form of message delivery; He sent His Son. The message is clear—God wants us to be sons also, not slaves or subjects but sons. In John 15:15 Jesus described this new identity by saying, "No longer do I call you slaves, for the slave does not know what his master is doing; but I have called you friends." With this new relationship, it is evident He wants us to be clued in on His plans. The Bible uses very distinct words for children or sons. The word *son* is not gender-specific, but relates to anyone who receives His Son.

Sons were recognized as those who carried on the family name and legacy. The word for "son" (*teknon*) means a small child, one who is totally dependent on a parent for sustenance but is in line for inheritance. The picture was to show that we are legitimate heirs but have some maturing to do before we are ready take on the responsibility of leading. The first thing a child must learn is submitting to authority and whom he can trust. Second, he will learn he is not to live only for himself— he is part of a larger family. We too have those same lessons to learn being a part of the family of God. Galatians 4:1–2 says, "Now I say that the heir, as long as he is a child [*teknon*], does not differ at all from a slave, though he is master of all, but is under guardians and stewards *until the time appointed by the father*" (NKJV). This verse is referring to Jesus as an example—how He was heir to everything, but while He was a child He was under tutors for the purpose of training for reigning.

You may be a born-again believer who is a son, but if you don't like the training and submission, then you will remain a *teknon* and will not be released at the appointed time of the Father. Part of the maturity of sons is to change the way we think and to trust His thoughts over our thoughts. We cannot assume the way we feel about another person or matter is the way our Father thinks about them. Maturity is understanding the nature of Him who has called us to be sons. Notice the progression in the term *sons*: "Because you are sons [huios], God has sent forth the Spirit of His Son into your hearts, crying out 'Abba, Father!'" (Galatians 4:6 NKJV). The term *son* changed to a more mature son, or perhaps we would say a young man who is strong and ready to represent the family name.

We don't give young children or toddlers the keys to the car and say, "Hey, go down to the store and get your own food." Obviously, we have no expectation of them having the wherewithal to accomplish that demand. I remember the first time my parents let me drive the family car by myself without anyone next to me telling me what to do. I felt that all of a sudden life had made a big turn for me and I could begin to think about what my future might look like. Maturity brings a new sense of identity, which changes how we view life.

Jesus asked His disciples who people thought He was. In Matthew 16:16, Peter spoke up and said, "You are the Christ, the Son of the living God" (NKJV). Jesus replied to Peter that flesh and blood did not reveal this to him but the Father who is in heaven. Then something unique happened; Jesus said to Peter, "You are Peter, and upon this rock I will build My church; and the gates of Hades will not overpower it. I will give you the keys of the kingdom of heaven" (Matthew 16:18-19). This was different because right before this He called Peter "Simon Barjona."

Simon means "wavering" or "sand." Up to this point, he was Simon or "shifting sand"; when he caught the revelation that Jesus was the Son of God, Jesus began to address him as Peter (*petros*) meaning "a piece of rock from a larger rock." Jesus was announcing to those listening that Peter was no longer known as shifting sand but he is now a chip off the old block. In the middle of this dialogue, Peter was given keys of the kingdom. Keys represent authority to bind what is bound in heaven and loose what has already been loosed in heaven. With the maturity of a son, our nature and the way we think grows into the opportunity to conduct business in the family name.

HEAD OR HEART

The first time I went to Africa I was 31 years old. I had knowledge of the Word, but I would soon find out if it was head or heart knowledge. I went to Kenya and Uganda, and on the last leg of a month-long trip we were in Ghana. I had already experienced levels of God's power but nothing like I would be facing. I was asked to preach to a meeting of ladies who were primarily wives of city government leaders. They were dressed in bright paisley colors, showing they viewed the event as special. After the preaching, a large crowd came forward to be filled with the Holy Spirit. As I and my brother Joe were making our way down the line, many were responding to the filling of the Spirit. I was summoned by a young man who was sent by another missionary to go and bring me to the other end of the line. I wasn't sure what the urgency was, so I told the boy I would be there in a moment but I was busy at the time. The little boy returned quickly only to tell me to come now. As I came near where a small crowd had formed I could see what the concern was. There was a young lady writhing up and down, side to side. Her tongue was moving in and out of her mouth like a serpent trying to detect the surroundings. I looked at the man who had invited us and I asked, "What is the problem?" He looked at me as if to say, *Can't you see what is going on here?* He told me that he had been trying to cast this demon out but it didn't budge. I could sense many watching were somewhat afraid. I had not seen anything quite like this. As soon as I mentioned that the Son of God had sent us to free this woman, the demon didn't like that, but the authority of Jesus backed by the blood of redemption gave this lady the right to be free. She fell backward and soon was baptized in the Holy Spirit.

Thinking like a son allows us to live like a son and have the authority of the Son of the Living God. First John 3:8-9 says, "For this purpose the Son of God was manifested, that *He might destroy the works of the devil.* Whoever has been born of God does not sin, *for His seed remains in him*; and he cannot sin, because he has been born of God" (NKJV).

GENERATIONAL SIN

Thinking like a son, we carry inside of us the same Spirit to destroy the works of the devil that Jesus walked in while He was on earth. The Bible teaches us, "Greater is He [Holy Spirit] who is in you than he who is in the world" (1 John 4:4). Sons of promise carry the seed of the resurrected Christ in us. God promised us in Genesis 3:15 that He has placed enmity (red hot hatred) between the seed of the woman and the seed of the serpent. We carry the seed that destroys the offspring of the devil and anything he brings against sons of the Kingdom of God.

Now read carefully what I am going to tell you. God has placed separation between these two seeds—the seed of the serpent and the seed of Christ. We hear people talking about "generational sin," and they try to tag every problem on bloodlines and family curses. I don't doubt that they are real. The truth is that the seed of Christ has crushed the head of the serpent. Another word for "generational sin" is *iniquity.* Iniquity means to bend toward or to have a propensity for something. If there is a history of alcoholism in your family, that is iniquity; it doesn't automatically pass on to you. The seed of iniquity can only move into your generation if you continue to agree with that iniquity through giving it a place. Some people give it a place by making excuses for the family even though they haven't been a practitioner of alcoholism. The mindset for those locked into generational sin is, "Well, I guess it's just the way life is and it's my lot in life and the family I was born into." As one thinks, so they become. If you continue to think like a son of iniquity, making excuses for the alcohol and pornography you are dealing with, they will stay in iniquity and will perpetuate the generational curse on your family.

A slave is one who is living without any expectancy of a future inheritance. A slave thinker just goes through the day without any reasoning of what they are working toward. A slave mindset is just trying to survive without any vision, and they have lost any desire for change. A generational slave carries only the thoughts that have been passed down to them from their family, and they are living out of the past and not from a proceeding word from God. I have known people who broke through the bonds of family iniquity, only for their family members to mock and ridicule their uppity thinking, when actually they are moving toward the destiny of sons. God has placed a part of Himself in all of us to be creative with godly imagination; but when generational iniquity is accepted as their reality, the god of this world (the devil, see 2 Corinthians 4:4) has blinded their minds—not their eyes, but their minds.

The devil knows that if he can control your mind and make you his son, then you will be kept a slave and your worldview will be very dark and angry. What turns a slave into a son is a father. For some, their thinking is rebellious due to some past experience with authority, and they have created inner vows that have become part of the fabric of their thinking. I know some who were mistreated by a leader or perhaps their biological father, and they built a structure of thoughts like I described in the beginning of this book. That structure of thought patterns began as a way to protect a broken heart or feelings of abandonment. After years of living from that fortress, it becomes normal. The problem is, it won't let anyone in and it won't let you out. Anyone who tries to get close is met with an angry barrage of words that you may not really mean, but it has become the only defense you trust. Though you may feel protected, you really are a slave to your own thoughts and perceptions that have become your reality.

Jesus was brought to this earth to place a bloodline of His own between you and the seed of the serpent. The serpent is known for whispering into your ear that no one cares and no one could ever love you and you are your own person. Allow Jesus to enter your heart right now and begin to dismantle the lies the devil has built up through generational lies that have passed on to you. You are of value to the family of God, and He wants to restore you to trust and to dream again. I know it won't be easy to let go of thoughts that you have believed for years were true. There are thoughts that may appear as facts but are not necessarily true. The devil uses half-truths to distort God's Word. Truth is not information; truth is a person called the Holy Spirit of truth. The fact may be that you have been deeply wounded; you may be one who has gone through a messy divorce and you now have feelings of revenge, but the truth will make you free even though the facts make you disappointed.

Being free means you are free to dream again and free to believe for the best to come to you. Blessing and cursing cannot come from the same fountain. Matthew 12:33 says, "Either make the tree good and its fruit good, or make the tree bad and its fruit bad; for the tree is known by its fruit." It's disappointing to expect good things to come to us while we are planting seed that makes the tree produce corrupt fruit. "Death and life are in the power of the tongue, and those who love it will eat its fruit" (Proverbs 18:21). The quickest way to start tearing down the fortresses of the mind is to start blessing. Blessing attracts life-giving things and cursing attracts dryness (see my book, *The Power of Blessing*). Sons of promise are those who have learned how to bless, and the slave mindset is set on cursing. Cursing is placing someone or something in a lower place than what God says about them. If you are speaking about someone in a way that is to lower them or demean them, then you have just cursed them. As you have said it about them, it is the same as saying it about the Lord. Jesus said "Inasmuch as you did it to one of the least of these My brethren, you did it to Me" (Matthew 25:40 NKJV).

ORPHAN THINKING

Jesus promised the disciples that He was going back to His Father, but He would not leave them as orphans (see John

14:17–18). Obviously, the disciples were not orphans who were homeless, but because He was leaving them they might feel abandoned. Jesus promised them another one like Him, who would be an advocate for them and lead them in the same way Jesus had led them. He was obviously referring to the Holy Spirit. Jesus told them it would be different because the Holy Spirit would not just be with them like Jesus had been, but the Holy Spirit was going to live inside of them.

Orphans you find in a third-world country are easy to spot. They are the ones who are least clothed and have their hands extended begging for some sustenance without any hope of a family inheritance. They are only looking to survive the day and be able to eat. In a spiritual sense, one can have a home and plenty of food and money but still have an orphan spirit and think like an orphan. They don't want covering with any accountability, and they are beggarly when it comes to under-standing that the Father in heaven wants to cover them and give them a hope and future. An orphan only hopes to get by without any vision for anything more. They are somewhat like a slave except they don't have any ties of accountability to any-one. Sons who have matured accept discipline because they know it leads to greater liberty and protection.

> *It is for discipline that you endure; God deals with you as with sons; for what son is there whom his father does not discipline? But if you are without discipline, of which all have become partakers, **then you are illegitimate children and not sons*** (Hebrews 12:7–8).

Paul is saying that if we refuse to accept discipline, then we are not His sons. The difference between being a son and illegitimate is the willingness to accept discipline. Illegitimate means that we don't have a family name or are not in line for a family inheritance. Our thinking can be like an orphan, while the Holy Spirit wants us to be born into the family of God.

FEELING LIKE AN ORPHAN

When I was about 16 years of age, I asked my mother if I could spend the night with my friend who lived across the street. I didn't ask Dad because he usually said "Whatever your mother thinks." I didn't realize that he wanted more authority that day for some reason. He called the neighbor's house about 11 o'clock that night and woke them up. "Is Kerry there?"

"Well, yeah, he's spending the night."

"You tell him to come home, now." I walked in the front door and Dad was standing behind the door with a belt in his hand. I didn't see it at first, and he said, "You didn't have permission to spend the night there."

I said, "Yeah, I did from Mom."

He said, "I said you didn't," and he grabbed my hand and swung the belt.

I grabbed the belt and had it wrapped around my hand, and I jerked it out of his hand. I said, "I think I'm a little too old for that now." And then I thought to myself, *What were you thinking? That was stupid.*

He just looked at me, and when I turned toward him, I saw he had a tear in his eye. I'd never seen my dad cry before. Then he said, in a quiet voice, "Go on to bed."

Man, I couldn't sleep. This was uncharted territory for me. Usually I took the spanking and it was all over except the stinging on my behind. It wasn't the spanking that I was missing. It was that tear that bothered me all night long. I was trying to figure out why I was feeling bad—I should have felt glad that I evaded the whipping. Even though I was right—because I had permission, or at least thought I did—I would rather have taken the chastisement than feel the way I was feeling. Finally it came to me—it was what I said to my dad that was bringing conviction to my soul. I refused him the right to discipline me, so I was in essence saying, "I am not your son." I was feeling like an orphan—like I no longer belonged to my father whom I loved dearly and who was very good to me.

The next morning at breakfast I said, "Dad." He was eating and not saying much. "I need to talk to you."

"Yeah, what."

"I'm so sorry for last night. If you just want to whip me right now it'd make me feel a lot better. Just put me out of my misery."

He said, "No, that's all right, but now you understand?"

I said, "Yes, sir. It was a misunderstanding. I'm sorry that I hurt you like that." I had never known what it felt like to be without the covering of a father, but that brief experience was enough for me.

HEARING AND OBEYING

"Although He was a Son, *He learned obedience* from the things which He suffered" (Hebrews 5:8). This verse is referring to Jesus, and you might wonder why Jesus would need to learn obedience; after all, He is the Son of God. Well, it's not obedience as we think of it—learning to behave and manners and all the things you learn as you mature. Like my story above, most of us probably suffered a few times before we learned to obey, but this is different. The lesson here is not dealing with rebellion but with passion. The word *suffer* here doesn't necessarily mean to be afflicted, but is the idea to be *deeply touched with compassion* to the point of feeling burdened. The next step for maturity of a son is to be able to be moved with compassion.

> *Then Jesus was led up by the Spirit into the wilderness to be tempted by the devil. And after He had fasted forty days and forty nights, He then became hungry. And the tempter came and said to Him, "If You are the Son of God, command that these stones become bread." But He answered and said, "It is written, 'Man shall not live on bread alone, but on every word that proceeds out of the mouth of God'"* (Matthew 4:1–4).

Before this in chapter 3 was Jesus's baptism. The dove came down and they heard a voice form heaven saying, *"This is My beloved Son, in whom I am well-pleased"* (Matthew 3:17). Immediately after this pronouncement, the Spirit led Him into the wilderness to confront the devil. As a Son, Jesus was setting precedent for how sons mature. *Jesus did not do any miracles until after the confrontation with the devil.* We as sons also will mature, not by what we go around but what we go through. Some people will say, "That was easy; it must have been a God thing," and if something is difficult we think it is the devil. The devil makes it easy to fall away. But when something is difficult He leads us through the wilderness.

Luke 4:14 says that Jesus came out of the wilderness after the temptation *"in the power of the Spirit."* Wasn't He already all-powerful? Though He held all power in His position, He showed all of His sons that if He overcame by speaking only the Word, we too have the same authority.

MY WILDERNESS

I have known for many years that I was called to preach. It was pretty cool when I was 17 and people would ask what I was going to be when I grew up. I would answer that I was going to preach. I am sure it sounded cute to those who asked. Well, one day something happened, and it wasn't so cool anymore. It moved from just something I said for identity to reality. My pastor sent me to a church he didn't know anything about, but he thought I was ready to leave the nest. It was a small church with a few elderly people who were divided. The previous pastor had been in affairs with three women in the church. Many of the folks still left were his family. I was not prepared for dealing with such moral decay. I would preach and people would make comments and shake their heads in disagreement. I had one announce out loud to the group that I couldn't preach. All confidence was shot, and now I was wandering in the wilderness without any support except the elder who had requested I come. After many hours of lying on the floor of the sanctuary, pleading with God to let me leave, one day I had breakthrough. He let me know why He allowed for me to come. I understood my assignment, and that helped me to endure the mocking I had to deal with. Later, things turned around, and we were able to install a new pastor with much more experience than I had. Having gone through a wilderness journey I can honestly say it was the school of the Spirit for me. All who knew me before would agree that I came out of the wilderness with greater authority than when I entered.

WE SHALL BE LIKE HIM

*Beloved, now we are children of God, and it has not **appeared** as yet what we will be. We know that when **He appears**, we will be like Him, because we will see Him just as He is* (1 John 3:2).

The word *appears* is used four times in eight verses. Each time, the intensity of the word increases. Most people read this verse and think, *One day when I get to heaven and see Jesus, I will be just like Him*—which is true. I suggest to you that we don't have to wait until we get to heaven. Notice, "when He appears." In the Greek, the word is *phanero,* which means "to make known." You can be like Him as you see Him now. The revelation that you receive will bring about the change in you to think like a son and live in the faith of the Son of God. The intensity of your relationship to the Son is the intensity with which you will live like the Son, using His name to cast out devils and healing the sick. We shall be like what we see in Him.

Jesus was summoned to come to Bethany because His friend Lazarus was sick (see John 11). Jesus told them that the sickness was not unto death but for the glory of God and that it was for the Son of God to be glorified. They knew Jesus as a healer and would not hear beyond their experience. The Bible says that Jesus stayed two more days where He was at the time. When He entered Bethany there were mourners and people coming to Jesus, saying, "If You had been, here Lazarus would not have died." The way He appeared to them, as a healer, was their level of intensity at that time. They didn't have the revelation of Him as the Resurrection and the Life. They were trying to explain to Jesus what *dead* meant. They even told Him, "Lazarus is now stinking from mortification."

If we could have revelation as mature sons of how wonderful and loving He is toward us, we could become like Him. Sons learn how to think like the resurrection and the life and how to speak life so we can be like Him. Just take a moment and ask the Holy Spirit to reveal Jesus the Son to you. That encounter will take an orphan spirit and give you identity that will increase your faith. "You know that He appeared in order to take away sins; and in Him there is no sin. No one who abides in Him sins; no one who sins has seen Him or knows Him" (1 John 3:5–6). If you are dealing with addictions and strongholds that you are finding difficult to get free from, ask the Holy Spirit to reveal Jesus the deliverer. As you will see, He is the one to set you free from the slavery of sin; then you will be like Him.

WEDDING PARABLE

Jesus used a parable in Matthew 22 to show the identity of those who belong to Him. The parable goes like this—a king had arranged a marriage for his son. He sent out his servants to call those who were invited. It was going to be a feast like no one had ever seen before. The guests mocked it, and one by one they started making excuses why they couldn't come. Some were too busy to bother to come—they were all caught up in their own lives. They soon began to mistreat the messengers who were delivering the invitations, and some they killed.

The king was furious and sent out his army and destroyed those who mistreated the messengers. Then the king sent the messengers out saying, "My feast is ready; invite anybody, no matter where they are." The day came and there were guests from every type of background and economic status. Everything was going as planned, but when the king came in to see his guests, he saw a man who was not wearing a wedding garment. The king went to the man and asked him why he came in without a wedding garment. The man had nothing to say, so the king quickly ordered him to be seized and thrown out of his presence into the darkness.

The parable speaks of Jesus coming to His own people and they did not accept Him as their Messiah. Then the invitation is extended to others who were not originally invited, which are the Gentiles or non-Jews—like many of us. When the king spots a man who is not properly dressed, the point of the parable becomes centered on who can enter into this Kingdom. My first thought was, *You invited him just the way he is, and now you are kicking him out?*

The culture of that time for weddings of such grandeur was for the host, or in this case the king, to furnish a wedding garment for each guest so everyone was covered with the same identity. Usually the garment would have the king's crest or insignia on the garment. The man who came in without the garment evidently did not want to be covered with the king's garment or to be identified as one of his. The story shows the thinking of our God and His Son Jesus. We come as we are, but then we are to be cleansed from all of the outside world's thinking and take on the identity of a son. Sons of God will have a renewed mind and be covered with the thoughts of God. The Spirit bearing witness inside says you're no longer a slave. You're no longer one who is cast away from your inheritance. You're not homeless and you're not an orphan. You have been bought and paid for by the blood of Jesus. You know deep down inside you, "I'm different. I'm different from the world. I'm different from what the culture is trying to pull me into, saying it's okay to do this or that sin. I'm different because I'm a member of the Kingdom of Light, a member of God's family. I'm led by the Spirit, not pushed by my feelings."

CREATION IS WAITING FOR SONS

Romans 8:14–17 says that those who are led by the Spirit are the sons of God, and we have received the Spirit of adoption whereby we cry out, "Abba, Father," or "Daddy!" We are now children of God, so He calls us to be heirs of His Kingdom and co-heirs with His Son Christ Jesus. God gave full authority to Adam to rule over creation. His job was to oversee what had already been created. The Bible says in Genesis 2:5 that there were no shrubs or plants in the fields yet because there had been no rain. The reason God had not released the rain was because man not been created and there was no one to cultivate the earth. Man was not made for creation; creation was made for man, and when the sons are not in place, things are not allowed to grow. Romans 8:19–20 says, "For the anxious longing of the creation waits eagerly for the revealing of the sons of God. For the creation was subjected to futility, not willingly, but because of Him who subjected it." When Adam fell, everything that he had oversight of became subjected to his failure. The devil took dominion over Adam and Eve and the creation that had been given to them to cultivate. *Cultivate* means "to bring to its full potential." Jesus came to not only redeem and buy back mankind with the payment of His blood but to also redeem everything that man lost through his disobedience. Jesus wants to redeem every part of our life. *Creation groans* waiting for the sons of God to step into our redemptive place and rule (see Romans 8:22), wearing the garment that identifies us as belonging to Him. The identifying mark of sons is that we are thinking like He thinks and we speak like He speaks. God is sovereign; He can do anything He wants to do, but He chooses to work through the sons of God. This is why He calls us co-heirs or co-creators. *We* don't create something that has never been created, but we can re-create and multiply what He has already spoken into creation.

> *Therefore if anyone is in Christ, he is a new creature; the old things passed away; behold, new things have come. Now all these things are from God, who reconciled us to Himself through Christ and gave us the ministry of reconciliation, namely, that God was in Christ reconciling the world to Himself, not counting their trespasses against them, and He has committed to us the word of reconciliation. Therefore, we are ambassadors for Christ, as though God were making an appeal through us; we beg you on behalf of Christ, be reconciled to God* (2 Corinthians 5:17–20).

Christ is in us as ambassadors, pleading through us for the world to be reconciled to God. God doesn't need us, but He chooses to wait for us to become mature sons with His mind, cultivating creation to come to its fullness, and I am glad He has allowed us to be a partner in redemption.

Chapter 9

LIVING AS GOD'S KINGDOM HEIRS

For everyone born of God overcomes the world. This is the victory that has overcome the world, even our faith (1 John 5:4 NIV).

We have the ability and power to overcome the world. Therefore, we have the ability and power to live as heirs of the Kingdom of God. There is more to being an heir than waiting around for the time to come when we gain an inheritance; there is work to be done. When Jesus was twelve years old He accompanied His parents to Jerusalem according to the custom of the feast (see Luke 2:42). When they concluded their time in Jerusalem His parents returned to their home, thinking Jesus was among the clan in the caravan. After a whole day journeying, they saw that He was not among their family, and they returned to Jerusalem. After three days, they found Him in the Temple sitting among the teachers, listening and asking questions. Those sitting among the group were astonished at His understanding. When His parents found Him, they said "Why have you done this to us?" You can imagine how panicked you would be as a parent if you lost your twelve-year-old son in an unfamiliar city. Jesus's answer is powerful; He said, "Why did you seek Me? Did you not know that *I must be about My Father's business?* (Luke 2:49 NKJV). Jesus was not referring to the carpentry business of Joseph, which He was probably learning, but *He was beginning to think like a Son.*

Being an heir is a call to join the family business. There is authority that comes with carrying the family name. We want to represent Him on earth as Jesus represents us in heaven. We are not to be lazy sons just waiting for inheritance day. One day we will go before the Judgment Seat of Christ where there will be a reward celebration for those who were faithful sons here on the earth, busy about the Father's business. Well, as sons we need to know what the Father's business is. Jesus said in Luke 19:10, "The Son of Man has come to *seek and to save* that which was lost." In Matthew 12:28, once again Jesus shows the family business, saying, "But if I *cast out demons* by the Spirit of God, then the kingdom of God has come upon you."

In John 5:7–9 Jesus visits the pool of Bethesda and finds a crippled man who had been there for many years. The hope that they had around the pool was that an angel came once each year and stirred the water and the first one in after the stirring would be healed. Jesus asked the lame man if he wanted to be healed. The man easily recited his mantra of why he could not be healed and totally missed what Jesus had asked. *Do you want to be healed?* Jesus healed the lame man and he took his pallet and walked away. The family business is to heal the sick, cast out demons, and bring the lost to salvation. The question is, what kind of sons are we? Being a co-heir means we share in His power and authority to be partners in the family business.

When I was a young boy attending elementary school, I would walk to school most days. The school was about a mile from my home. Near the school was a small grocery store named Eddie Moore Grocery. There were no chain stores then, only the typical mom-and-pop store. My dad arranged with the owner that I would come by in the morning and charge my lunch money, which was 30 cents. Then in the afternoon on the way home, I was allowed to go by the store and get a snack or candy. One afternoon my friend was walking with me and went into the store with me and observed my protocol. I picked out my candy selection and placed it on the counter, and Mr. Moore wrote out a ticket and I signed my dad's name. My friend proceeded to do the same. Mr. Moore told him that would be 20 cents. My friend looked puzzled and said, "I want to do what Kerry did."

Mr. Moore said to him "I know his father, but I don't know yours." I felt sorry for my friend; it was as if he was an orphan.

Sons who serve in the Kingdom of God carry the name of their father, and hell knows that as well. Demons know the mark of the blood, just like in Exodus 12 when the Hebrew slaves took the blood of a lamb and placed it over the doors of their homes. When judgment came through the land, the death angel (*abaddon*—destroyer) passed through Egypt, and every home that was marked by the blood, the destroyer passed over. Much in the same way, today demons recognize when a house is marked by the blood covenant of Christ. When we use the family name of Jesus, the spirit of destruction must move aside. You are sent to do business in the name of one who has raised the dead and healed the sick and has power over darkness. You are a son who is at work in Father's business. If we are not going to serve, we may still be a son, but a son without power. I don't need power to do nothing. I need the power of the Holy Spirit to do business in this Kingdom. This is why we pray, "Your kingdom come. Your will be done, on earth as it is in heaven" (Matthew 6:10).

LET THERE BE LIGHT

In Genesis 1, the Father, the Son, and the Holy Spirit are present, and the very first thing they dealt with was the darkness. The Hebrew word for "darkness" in that context is *khoshek*, which means "darkness you can feel" as in tangible misery. I've been down in the catacombs in Kiev, Ukraine, where it is so dark that I could literally feel its thickness. Even though there was a little bit of light, I could feel the darkness tangibly, and it felt really eerie. "The earth was without form, and void; and darkness was on the face of the deep. ...Then God said, 'Let there be light'; and there was light" (Genesis 1:2–3 NKJV). Not until verse 16 of Genesis 1 did God create the sun, the moon, and the stars. So where did light come from in verse 3 if they were not placed by God until after He created the land and the waters and the seeds, grass, and fruit trees?

I believe God was speaking to Himself. He was confronting the prince of darkness or the absence of God's presence. Remember, Lucifer was cast down to a planet of darkness. God said *let there be light* just as He later was speaking to the

Godhead and said, "Let Us make man in Our image" (Genesis 1:26). When He said *let there be light*, I believe He unveiled Himself and darkness was pushed out. This is the very thing God is continually doing—Christ in us is pushing back the darkness. The devil is afraid of the glory the sons of God carry by virtue of His resurrection.

Some people can discern what the demonic realm is doing more than they can discern what the presence of God is doing. They can tell you more of what the devil is doing than what God's doing because it's much easier to sense the demonic realm, as it is part of our fallen nature and surrounds us daily. But we have to press past the suspicion and the cynicism and all of those feelings to be able to sense the presence of God. It's amazing how suspicious we can get and blame God for that. It's not difficult to sense when someone doesn't like you because that's just part of the fallen nature we have to deal with. But some say, "The Lord showed me they don't like me." Why would God show you that? What glory is in that to you? In fact, He reveals on a need-to-know basis. If you don't need to know, you don't get to know. So if you don't need to know and you're still getting thoughts like that, you're still plugged in to the wrong source. His thoughts to us are about Himself, not about someone else and what they may be thinking.

HE HAS SENT ME

Jesus stood up in the Temple and opened the Scriptures to Isaiah 61:1–3 and begin to read. It was a Messianic prophecy concerning Him. The prophecy was that the Spirit of the Lord would be upon Messiah to anoint Him to preach good news (the gospel), to heal the brokenhearted, to proclaim the prison doors opened to captives, and to preach the acceptable year of the Lord, which was Jubilee. He was comfort for those in mourning and gave the oil of joy for mourning. After reading this publicly, Jesus said, "Today this Scripture has been fulfilled in your hearing" (Luke 4:21). Jesus quoted every part of Isaiah 61 except the day of our God's vengeance. This is significant showing that *He didn't come to pronounce judgment, but to declare healing and freedom of the nation.* Jesus was announcing the New Covenant was coming and the day when the final price of redemption was to be paid.

Jesus described the family business precisely, even down to what we should leave out. Preach deliverance and salvation but not condemning. There will be a time when judgment will occur at the Great White Throne Judgment. Today we are preaching from the mercy seat of Christ. After Noah built the Ark and the rain and water tables of the deep begin to erupt, it was God who shut the door on the Ark, not Noah. I believe it was a prophetic sign to show it is God who decides when the final door of salvation will be shut, not man. In my thinking, God didn't want Noah to see the judgment that was coming, but that Noah was only to see God as the deliverer. Noah rode out the judgment while floating on top of the flood.

The Kingdom of God is the family business, and the gifts of the Spirit are the tools of the family business. The gifts were not given so we could play games with them. They're not to be used as spooky or strange. The gifts of the Spirit are spiritual abilities to carry out the work of our family business. So when Jesus said, "I'm showing you the Father," then Philip understood and knew his destiny in God the Father (see John 14:8–14). Every son knows that they will be like their father.

We can't get to the Father unless we come through His Son. If you know the Father, you know the Son. If you know the Son, you know the Father. That is why God wants to raise up mature sons and daughters so the whole world will know the Father. When they've seen us, they've seen the Father. When they've been around us, they can say, "This is what God's kindness looks like. This is what the love of God feels like." Hebrews 3:6 says, "Christ was faithful as a Son over His house—whose house we are, if we hold fast our confidence." The writer of Hebrews sees us as the house of Christ.

In John 14:2, Jesus says, "In My Father's house are many *mansions*; if it were not so, I would have told you" (NKJV). *Mansions* is not the best translation for this verse. The original says *places* or *rooms*. He's speaking about a very wealthy father who had a large compound and the whole family had separate houses built within the walls of the compound. We could read it like this, "In my Father's house, who I am, there are many rooms and places." I think sometimes we put up signs on the doors of our heart and say "no trespassing." Some people will compartmentalize their relationship with Jesus. They have a room for Sunday when they bring Him out and worship, and then Monday they place Him in the back room unless there happens to be a midweek crisis, at which time they will call for Jesus to come out. Others who have friends who don't know Jesus, will hide Jesus until their friends leave. Unlike a secular job, the family business is a 24-hour-a-day life that doesn't have closed and sealed rooms or time clocks. Our public anointing is only as strong as our private hidden times are. When we invited Jesus into our house, it must be *"Mi casa, su casa."* When He comes in, He takes over all the rooms; it's called the infilling of the Holy Spirit.

VIOLENT TAKE IT

Matthew 11:12 says, "From the days of John the Baptist until now the kingdom of heaven suffers violence, and violent men take it by force." There have been many messages preached around this passage with the main point being violent and radical. The word for "violent" is *biadzo,* which means "to crowd out." John the Baptist preached about the Kingdom but never did enter into the Kingdom. Jesus was the door to the Kingdom, and John preached the preparation to receive the King of the Kingdom. *Biadzo* means that when this King enters, *He crowds out everything that is not of His making.* Here is a picture of what *biadzo* would be—picture a glass half full of dirt. As water is filling the glass, the dirt is displaced and crowded out and the only thing left is the water. The greater the filling of the water of the Word and the greater the infilling of the Holy Spirit, the more crowding occurs, until there are no more gray areas of mixture. Doubt and unbelief have no place to stay.

INCREASE OUR FAITH

Galatians chapter 4 is all about sonship in Christ; it really gives us insight into how God thinks about this concept. When I first started pastoring my son Kevin was just a toddler. He would run through the church waiting for me to leave. Someone made the comment that the pastor's child was running in the church. I came and took Kevin's hand, and that person said, "That's what PKs do"—as if to say pastor's kids are expected to be different and break the rules.

I asked, "What's a PK?"

"Pastor's kid."

And I said, "He doesn't know he's a PK. He just knows I'm Daddy." PK could just as well be a plumber's kid.

Sometimes we label people and put them in restrictive categories that squelch their true identities. We need to assume our roles as *huios*—mature sons and heirs of the Kingdom of God: "God has sent forth the Spirit of His Son into our hearts, crying, 'Abba! Father!' Therefore *you are* no longer a slave, but a son; and if a son, then *an heir* through God" (Galatians 4:6–7). You are not in a class of society, you are in the Kingdom; and you are not labeled by your socioeconomic status, your Daddy is the King.

The apostles had asked Jesus to increase their faith in Luke 17:5–10. I am sure they felt noble by asking for something that would be beneficial. Perhaps they thought Jesus would pray over them or lay hands on them and impart the gift of faith. Instead, Jesus taught them two parables. He said:

> *Which of you, having a slave plowing or tending sheep, will say to him when he has come in from the field, "Come immediately and sit down to eat"? But will he not say to him, "Prepare something for me to eat, and properly clothe yourself and serve me while I eat and drink; and afterward you may eat and drink"? He does not thank the slave because he did the things which were commanded, does he?* (Luke 17:7–9)

The lesson seems cruel from our standards today, but the message is clear. Remember, the question was, "How do I increase my faith?" The first thing we should know is that faith has levels and room for us to grow in. Second, Jesus was saying to them if you only do the minimal that is expected, faith will not increase. For sons to grow in faith, we must exceed doing just enough to get by. Faith is not belief. Belief can be more analytical—from the head. Faith exceeds belief because it acts on what it believes. Belief says it's possible, and we continue to discuss all the facets of what we believe. Faith without works is dead according to James 2:20. Increasing faith is rarely comfortable because it takes you down paths that you don't have a grid for. We call it stretching faith, because it pulls on the anointing in you to a point of being somewhat uncomfortable with the uncharted waters.

My first real stretch in faith was at about 20 years of age. I was faithful in my local church. There were four of us young men who were preparing for the ministry. We talked a good game about what we would do when we were thrust out into full-time preaching, as we called it then. It was more fun to talk about and dream about than when it happened. My pastor's wife came to me and said, "I want you to take my class of the adults that meets in the sanctuary before the service." I went into a stare and asked her to repeat the statement. She laughed and said slowly what I thought she had said but was hoping it was a mistake. She gave the details and said, "It's time for you to step into your calling."

The class she mentioned was the older adults, including my mother and sister. They were seasoned, red-meat carnivores (see 1 Corinthians 3:2). My faith went from being a little arrogant about the call to "I don't know if I am called." On Saturday night I was always up to early hours praying and pleading with God to give me a nugget. I would not go to sleep until I had that nugget from God. I taught that class up until the time I left to pastor a church. The experienced forced me like nothing else would to study with depth of heart. It was very uncomfortable in the beginning, and my faith was sorely stretched, but I had to learn to trust the Holy Spirit for the times I did not know what to say. I was quickly emptied of myself and all the junk was crowded out. It was a prelude for what I would do the rest of my life. I am not sure the course my life would have taken if fear had the upper hand and I had taken the easy way out and declined the invitation to grow. When we only do what is the minimal and comfortable, faith is not increased.

LOVE VERSUS LABOR

Jesus said, "If you love Me, you will keep My commandments" (John 14:15)—not out of the fear of hell but out of a love relationship. God has given us the power to resist the temptations of the devil—He has given us love that is stronger than the pull of sin. John 1:1 says, "In the beginning was the Word [the Son], and the Word [the Son] was with God, and the Word was God." In other words, you can't separate the Word from the Son of God; He was in the beginning, God.

> *All things came into being through Him, and apart from Him nothing came into being that has come into being. In Him was life, and the life was the Light of men* (John 1:3-4).

In Matthew 5:14, Jesus tells us that we are "the light of the world." And in John 1:5 Jesus is described: "The Light shines in the darkness, and the darkness did not comprehend it." John 1:12 says, "But as many as received Him, to them He gave the right to become children of God, even to those who believe in His name." Now, because He's given us the right and the authority to become sons and daughters, He's not calling us to be servants. He's not calling us to serve Him out of the fear of hell. He's calling us to be a partner in this life with Him. Though the Head of this Kingdom is in heaven, His Body is moving and carrying out the family business.

Luke 15:11–32 gives a contrast between two sons. The parable is known as the prodigal son, but it is not just about one son but two. The elder brother is known for his faithfulness to the family farm, and the younger brother, the one labeled the prodigal, appears to be hasty and wanting to test his mettle out in the world. The younger son requests an advance of his inheritance. By our culture this would seem unusual because his father was still alive. In Jewish culture, parents gave their children an inheritance while they were alive to help them invest their legacy. His father divided equally between his two sons. The younger left for a far country. He spent his wealth on loose living, and when a famine hit the land he found himself in need for the first time in his life. He got work—feeding pigs—and would even eat their food. One day while feeding the hogs he came to his senses, which means his thoughts as a son retuned. He realized that even the servants of his father were treated better and had plenty to eat. He decided it would be better to be a servant in his father's house than be on his own and hungry. He returned to his father, who had been keeping an eye open for his son's return (fathers are always looking for prodigals). He told his father that he was willing to be a servant, but the father didn't demote him, he received him as a son. He restored him with his robe and a ring, giving him the identity of his father.

Here is where the contrast of the elder brother comes in. The elder brother heard the noise of the party and was told, "Your brother who was thought dead has come home." It made him furious, and he refused to go to the party because he compared himself to his brother. He was the faithful son who had been laboring hard to please his father and had never been disobedient or wasteful like this younger one. Jealousy probably set in because he worked for his father but never really knew his heart. When asked by his father why he was upset, he said, "You never gave me a fatted calf or a party." His father shared his heart as a father: "My son whom I thought was lost has come home." But he said, "You have always been with me and everything I have has been yours." The elder brother could have had a party any time he wanted, but because he was a son with a slave mentality he lost a lot of time of joy and love from his father.

It's possible to be so busy working for God that we are not able to enjoy His love. When there are legalistic thoughts and rules that separate you from Him then *you might be a son in the house but not a son with promise.* The elder brother was living in the house near his father without any joy, whereas the *prodigal was living outside of the house and yet he was still a son, but a son without the protection and benefits of a son.* You may know someone who says they are a believer in Christ but lives like a pig; you can tell them they may be a son, but it doesn't help when you live under a covering other than Father's house. You never have to worry about food or protection in Father's house. *If you are away from God, just know that He is watching for you to make the move toward Him and come home. He won't reject or make you feel shame over the past. Today is a new day and a time to make a fresh start.*

Chapter 10

JUST AS WE ARE ONE

On one of my trips to South Korea I had been teaching on the power of blessing. The following Monday a group of church leaders were going to gather for the express purpose of being unified over North Korea's missile launches into the Sea of Japan. The threat was very real, and some of the launches came close to the mainland. Originally the plan was get into agreement and curse the leader of North Korea. After hearing about blessing, they changed their tactics and did what the Bible said to do to your enemies, which was to bless them. It seemed strange at first, and then they felt the pleasure of God on them which flowed out of them like a river. The day of the next launch, something happened and the launch failed to take place. Unity is when we agree with God, not just one another. We can get agreement on things we all want but it may not be unity. Unity is not uniformity, but it is knowing what God is saying and moving in concert with Him.

*That they **may all be one**; even as You, Father, are in Me and I in You, **that they also may be in Us**, so that the world may believe that You sent me. The glory which You have given Me I have given to them, **that they may be one, just as We are one**; I in them and You in Me, that they may be **perfected in unity**, so that the world may know that You sent Me, and **loved them, even as You have loved Me**. Father, **I desire** that they also, whom You have given Me, be with Me where I am, so that they may see My glory which You have given Me, for You loved Me before the foundation of the world* (John 17:21–24).

This passage from John 17 is called a high priestly prayer that Jesus prayed for His disciples and us before He ascended. He was praying that *we would be one with Him and the Father.* The glory of God is a great unifier. We can never really unite people, but the glory of God can. It's the unity of the Spirit, not the unity of people. Unity is somewhat different than agreement. Agreement is saying the same thing. We could possibly have everyone parroting the same thing and have agreement that sounds like unity, but then eventually we start breaking into personal agendas and preferences. Unity is different in that it happens in a person's spirit. It's not the unity of people, but it's the uniting of our spirit with the Spirit of God.

When Jesus the Son of God says, "Father I desire for them to have what We have together," you know it's going to be answered. Jesus is explicitly saying that His disciples are examples of the sons He is raising up. Some He even calls the *sons of thunder.* Then He goes on to say, "O righteous Father, although the world has not known You, yet I have known You; and these have known that You sent Me; and I have made Your name known to them, and will make it known, so that the love with which You loved Me may be in them, and I in them" (John 17:25–26). Jesus is saying that the very thing that His Father gave Him when He came to this earth—the love of God and the glory of God—He in turn gives it to the sons of God. These are essential, vital ingredients we need to operate here on earth. When Jesus appeared to His disciples, He said, "'Peace be with you; as the Father has sent Me, I also send you.' And when He had said this, He breathed on them and said to them, 'Receive the Holy Spirit'" (John 20:21–22).

Jesus was not giving them just a nice pat on the back and breathing "Atta boys" to His disciples on the way out. He gave them the very power He operated with for three and a half years. "Here is the *love of the Father*, the *glory of the Father*, the Holy Spirit, and now I'm giving to you the same empowerment that I had while on the earth. Go and make disciples." It wasn't about sitting in a classroom giving people theories; it was about personally revealing the glory of God so they could experience the unveiling of the heart of the Father. Jesus said, "All things for which you pray and ask, believe that you have received them, and they will be granted you" (Mark 11:24). We are one with Christ. Believe that you have it—that's not wishful thinking and hoping it all works out. I love when my wife prays. She says, "We're not going to have that." She's not talking to me. She says, "We're pushing back. We're going after this." She's deliberate in her prayers. She doesn't pray, "Thy will be done, oh God." She knows His will and it's going to be done because it carries the authority. The psalmist tells us in Psalm 37:4, "Delight yourself in the Lord; and He will give you the desires of your heart." Believe it! The word *delight* means to lean into. Lean into Him in prayer and He will hear you.

MOVING AS ONE

Whenever they moved, they moved in any of their four directions without turning as they moved. As for their rims they were lofty and awesome, and the rims of all four of them were full of eyes round about. Whenever the living beings moved, the wheels moved with them. And whenever the living beings rose from the earth, the wheels rose also (Ezekiel 1:17–19).

Ezekiel describes this unusual sight as a wheel inside a wheel. Each one of these creatures looked fierce, each moving in concert with the one leading, and when they changed direction none would turn their heads but only looked forward. None of the four would break rank, and they didn't seem to be bothered when the direction would change and they were not leading any more. Though the direction changed at times, the mission stayed intact. None of them were trying to promote what they were facing. This is such a perfect picture of what Jesus was conveying before His ascension. The unity of the Spirit means that the Spirit is at the center giving the instructions for when and where the wheel was to turn. If there is not unity and we are hearing different directions, we will tear apart and only our own strength will be left. When there is unity, the strength is multiplied fourfold in four directions.

Isaiah 65:8 "As the new wine is found in the cluster, and one says, 'Do not destroy it, for there is benefit in it,' so I will act on behalf of My servants in order not to destroy all of them." The message here is the cluster. When a grape is pulled from the cluster it dries up and there is no juice for wine to be made from it—it becomes a dried-up raisin. There is blessing, meaning wine, in the cluster. Wine represented the Holy Spirit to come upon the Body of Christ, or we could say the "Cluster of Christ." The anointing is inside the cluster when there is a union with Christ and unity of the Spirit. Many times I have seen a strong anointing on someone, and instead of staying connected to the vine where the anointing flowed from, they ventured out only to end up a raisin with only stories from past moves of God. The power is in the center of God's will, not around the soft edges of being a celebrity.

> *Behold, how good and how pleasant it is for brothers to dwell together in unity! It is like the precious oil upon the head, coming down upon the beard, even Aaron's beard, coming down upon the edge of his robes. It is like the dew of Hermon coming down upon the mountains of Zion; for there the Lord commanded the blessing—life forever* (Psalm 133:1–3).

This is a great verse when describing how God views unity. This was a psalm of ascent, meaning it was one of the Psalm that was sung or chanted as the people would climb the stairs going up to the magnificent Temple Solomon had built. God has a sense of smell—obviously not like ours, but unity must have an aroma because it was pleasant like the anointing oil that was poured over the High Priest, which was Aaron. This oil moved from his head down to the skirts of this special robe with bells and pomegranates alternating. The hem of the robe was the most saturated part of his robe. It reminds me of the woman who had the issue of blood for many years, and she pressed through the crowd to reach Jesus because she said within herself, "If I could just touch the hem of Jesus's garment I will be healed." This picture of unity releases healing. The oil was special and could only be used for dedicating the utensils used in the Temple or on the priest, preparing him to enter the Holy of Holies. Unity has an aroma, and the High Priest is a type of Christ. Hebrews calls Him our Apostle and High Priest of our confession. The unity or anointing oil was coming down from the Head of the Body of Christ to us, becoming more saturated at the bottom of His garment. Here is the kicker to this message—where the unity was, there God said, "I will command blessing." He didn't say just wherever there are folks saying the same thing, but there. There is a special place. It's a place where you go; it's a place of destination because it doesn't come to you. *You have to make a point to go there.*

It was 1994, and a special move of refreshing had begun to fall on my congregation and me. It was such a sweet rain from heaven. Many people found refreshing and healing. They came with all kinds of brokenhearted issues and abandonment issues only to find the love from God our Father. The river, as we called it, was flowing. People were driving from outside of the area to get a drink. The sweet aroma of unity was indescribable. One lady in particular would visit regularly. She told me, "I was praying that the Lord would send the river my direction where I was attending church," but to her surprise the Lord said to her rather straightforwardly, "If you're thirsty, you go to the river there." She did exactly that and was there for many years. The word *commanded* in the above verse is a Hebrew word, *tsavah*. It means *to send a specific message that is direct and personal.* It's not a "whosoever" but is specific to the place of unity. God said that one of the seven things He hates, which are abominations to Him, is one who spreads strife (division) among the brethren (see Proverbs 6:19). We need to pick up on how God thinks—*He loves the aroma of unity and hates the scent of division.* The reason the devil works through those who sow the opposite of unity is he knows God will remove Himself from among divisive people, which removes any power or authority against wickedness.

THE ART OF THE APOTHECARY

On a return flight from Europe I was between flights at Heathrow International Airport. Just wanting to find a gift for Diane, I found a perfume store. This wasn't just a place that sold perfume, as I was informed rather quickly, it was a perfumery. I found out that I was not too much up on the world of perfumery. The idea was to select different scented oils, and the perfumer would blend them in the right amounts to create a perfume that would be unique—not another perfume in the world like yours. I was feeling very creative, and I must admit a little like a mad scientist. I gathered all the ingredients with the help of my apothecary. When it came time for the special chemistry to take shape, the one assisting said to me, somewhat puzzled, "Is this concoction for you?"

I said back, somewhat puzzled, "Well, no, it's for my wife."

She realized that I was a rookie at the finer things of life and said, "Sir, I must match the oils to her body for the right chemistry because everyone is different and it will react with her body chemistry differently than yours." I felt a little embarrassed and left empty-handed. Having time to ponder my new lesson in perfumery I realized how beautiful it is to see how He matches His aroma of unity with the Body He has commanded His blessing upon.

UNITY IN THE INNER MAN

Unity cannot be achieved by some external focus; no leader is able to make unity appear simply by trying to keep people happy or busy. Unity is born of the Spirit of God. Without a renewed mind, division will emerge and sometimes from the most unlikely sources. When an individual doesn't know how God thinks about them it's easy to start thinking about what they suspect others are thinking about them, when in all actuality they are not thinking about them at all. There is power in right thinking, which better enables us to live in the unity of the Spirit.

> *So that Christ may dwell in your hearts through faith; and that you, being rooted and grounded in love, may be able to comprehend with all the saints what is the **breadth and length and height and depth**, and to know the love of Christ which surpasses knowledge, that you may be **filled up to all the fullness of God*** (Ephesians 3:17–19).

When unity has been rooted into the fabric of a person or congregation, revelation goes to another level. The mind is renewed to know God with fresh insight. The preaching is not only inspirational, it becomes transformational. Faith is moving inside of you at a fast pace, and prayers that took seemingly longer to be answered are happening as quickly as you can ask. The power of agreement doesn't have to be asked for; it's there automatically and the heavens are open. This would be called a move of God, but really it is the unity of God. The Spirit is always willing; it is the flesh that is weak and wants to be elevated.

There is a promise in the above verses we need to lock on and contend for. This unity of the Spirit will not only unify but will also cause love to be rooted and grounded. The prerequisite for unity to transform a place is that love is starting to grow and sprouting roots, which give it depth and longevity. When something is rooted, it is able to draw water and nutrients from the depths below and not just survive from surface sustenance. When love becomes rooted it will be able to weather the occasional ripple that rises up without any confusion or disturbance. The promise we are given is that there would be width and length and depth and height for the purpose of being filled with all the fullness of God. The word for "fullness" is *pleroo*, which means "spilling over, no more capacity for anything else." The fullness of God is not one-dimensional but has width and length, which are linear, but then it goes deep and high. The natural eye has difficulty seeing four dimensions. However, with a renewed mind we can see through the mind of the Spirit fully. We were created in God's imagination, and with the renewed mind our God-given imagination is able to see without limits. Stephen could see into heaven while he was being stoned. What he saw was Jesus giving him a standing ovation at the right side of the Father. Stephen was able to forgive those stoning him—people he had known—because he was no longer seeing one-dimensionally. Length and width thinkers can only see the rejection and pain of the situation. The fullness of God allows us to see with depth and height and be able to look past the purpose of the devil and see the goodness of God. The Bible says the eye of the Lord goes to and fro across the earth looking for those who are full of faith (see 2 Chronicles 16:9).

"Now to Him who is able to do far more abundantly beyond all that we ask or think, *according to the power that works within us*" (Ephesians 3:20). This verse is in continuity with the above verse of fullness. A renewed mind moves beyond what one could only ask or think; it is limited only by the power that is operating in him. This really excites me to think that unity of the Spirit unlocks greater dimensions of visibility into the power of God and the same anointing is working in us. The sky is the limit! How far can you see? We have to train our minds to know what our spirits already know. The spirit is willing; the flesh is not so cooperative. Our flesh is viewed as the mind, will, and intellect. But our spirits are very much alive and strong; even while we're asleep God is downloading to us (see Psalm 16:7). *I believe that our spirit knows everything there is to know about God.* So I have to train my mind to submit to what my spirit is saying. So when a situation arises that is critical, upsetting, or bothersome, we either operate as sons or slaves. The first response depends on the authority we step into. A servant says, "Here we go again. I knew that was going to happen." Sons step into every situation thinking, "All things work for good to me because I am a son called to the family business."

RELEASE OF THE INNER MAN

Therefore we do not lose heart, but though our outer man is decaying, yet our inner man is being renewed day by day (2 Corinthians 4:16).

The outward part of us obviously is our physical body, which has an expiration date on it. Every day we put mileage on this body and we keep record by age. We also have a middleman—our soul, or some call it their will. The middleman definitely gets stuck in the middle at times. The will has the final say even though our spirit is shouting out instructions. A mature son has learned how to work between the soul and the spirit. We need an intellect to function here in this life. The soul only sees analytically in linear thought, but the inner man can see without time and space. Verse 18 in this chapter says that what is seen is temporal, and what is not seen is eternal. Our soul and body are temporal, but the inner man is eternal and is being renewed daily. As time goes on our inner man, the deepest part of our being, is becoming more like what Adam had before the fall of man. Galatians 2:20 explains this transformation like this: "I have been crucified with Christ; and it is no longer I who live, but Christ lives in me; and the life which I now live in the flesh I live by faith in the Son of God, who loved me and gave Himself up for me." The old man of the soul was crucified with Christ—it is no longer the dominant force in my life—but now the life I am to live is out of the inner man, Christ being the dominant voice. The message here is for the inner man to be released, who sees things from being seated in heavenly places. The inner man is less likely to get offended and lose sight of the kingdom of God.

Chapter 11

AWAKENING THE DREAMER IN YOU

B y the very act of creation there is a degree of the dreamer in all of us. I am not only referring to the dream where you are asleep and have picture thoughts. I am thinking more like the ability to see a future desire. Imagination is closely related to dreaming, so I will use these two terms interchangeably in this chapter. Imagination is narrowly defined as "the act or power of forming a mental image or picture of something not yet present." Albert Einstein said, "Imagination is more important than knowledge." Allan Kay said, "The best way to predict the future is to create it." These famous people had one thing in common—they were dreamers of things that were not tangible but were real in the world of their imagination. To a dreamer, all things are possible because they believe outside of their natural senses. If they could imagine it, then it exists at least in some dimension. The Internet was built upon a series of thoughts and dreams and imaginations that led to things happening at the speed of light and faster than the speed of sound. It all began unseen to most, but seen by those who had a desire to see the unseen.

The Holy Spirit wants to awaken the unseen inside all of us. "For as he thinks within himself, so he is" (Proverbs 23:7). All of the successful ones took a dream of their own, or in some cases they picked up the dream that others stopped believing in and saw it to fulfillment. Dreamers who are successful are very focused and not easily derailed from the target they have set for themselves. They are visionaries who are usually way before their time; they are not waiting until someone agrees with what they are seeing. In many cases, they would be called the outliers of their day, and we are glad they are because it brings some great inventions and medical breakthroughs.

"Where is no vision, the people are unrestrained" (Proverbs 29:18). In other verbiage we would say, *When there is no ability to see into the future, people have no moorings to tie their lives to.* There must also be those of us who buy into those visions and get on board to work toward the optimum end. If there were no dreamers and visionaries, there would be no work to do. Those who think outside the box help create the box that others can work inside of. Some think in abstract terms, while others need the known to create the unknown. Either way, we need one another and the creativity that is innate in all of us. The key as we will explore in this chapter is how to unlock this dreamer/imagination in us.

YOUR SONS AND DAUGHTERS WILL PROPHESY

In Acts 2, on the day of Pentecost the Holy Spirit suddenly came into that upper room. Tongues of fire were visibly sitting upon the 120 who had stayed. They believed what Jesus had said—the promise of the Father was coming. The promise was the inheritance that the firstborn sons customarily distributed to the family. Jesus was the Firstborn (see Romans 8:29). After Jesus ascended into heaven and received His inheritance, He then distributed to the rest of the family through the outpouring of the Holy Ghost. The power of the Holy Spirit changed the whole world that day and continues on through the present. Peter stood up to give some foundation to what was happening, because there were those thinking that these people looked like drunks on a Saturday night. Peter explained by saying they weren't drunk because it was only the third hour of the day (nine in the morning). They had not had enough time to get drunk even if they wanted to. Peter carried great wisdom by referring back to the prophecy that was found in the writings of Joel the prophet. Joel 2:28 says, "I will pour out My Spirit on all mankind; and your sons and daughters will prophesy, your old men will dream dreams, your young men will see visions."

It is important to note here that Peter didn't say that the Holy Spirit came to give gifts of the spirit. This was later introduced into the church through Paul in First Corinthians. The outpouring Peter was seeing was releasing the power to prophesy, which is forthtelling and dreams and visions. All of this was pointing toward the release of the creativity we were originally created with. God gave us a part of Himself when He breathed into man. The God of the universe gave us the ability to see beyond ourselves. The Holy Spirit in you is for much more than occasional comforting. He wants us to see what He sees so we can partner with Him in the family business. "What things soever ye desire, when ye pray, believe that ye receive them, and ye shall have them" (Mark 11:24 KJV). *Desire* means "to see or picture with the end in mind, pray." We have all prayed prayers without thinking of what we would like to see. If we are co-heirs, or we could say co-creators together with Him, then we need to pray what He wants us to see. He is praying through us (see Romans 8:26), so there should be an agreement with Him to bring to earth what has originally been in heaven. Jesus said, "I only do what I see the Father do" (see John 5:19). So we should also, as sons, do what we see Him doing. We can pray and ask the Lord to unlock our inner man, our spirit, so we can see what to do through dreams, visions, and prophecy.

TAKE A PICTURE

I pray that the eyes of your heart may be enlightened, so that you will know what is the hope of His calling, what are the riches of the glory of His inheritance in the saints (Ephesians 1:18).

This is sometimes referred to as an apostolic prayer. Paul is asking for the eyes of our heart, not the eyes of our head, to be enlightened. The word *enlightened* changes the strength of this passage. The word is *photizo*—we get our English word *photograph* from this word. We could read the text as, "I pray your spiritual eyes would be able to take a picture of your calling and the inheritance that is glorious." Part of the outpouring of the Holy Spirit would anoint our eyes to have a picture of what we are going to be doing. He really does want us to be able to see the lame walking and the blind seeing. Allowing the Holy Spirit to give you a graphic look at what He has in store for you will help keep you focused on the glory to come. A man with a theory is at the mercy of a man with a picture. *A thousand words can create a picture, and one picture can create ten thousand words.*

We remember more of what we see than what we hear. Jesus being crucified is a picture that will never leave my memory. Many times while praying for someone, the Holy Spirit would remind me of that picture; without saying anything, I would experience a power surge. Our position may affect what we see. Ephesians 2:6 says that we are *seated with Him in heavenly places* in Christ Jesus. Psalm 1:1 says, "How blessed is the man who does not walk in the counsel of the wicked, nor stand in the path of sinners, *nor sit in the seat of scoffers!*" Where we sit in life can skew or improve our ability to see where we are going. The heavenly place has the advantage of being above the drama of life with a better perspective. The seat of the scornful is someone who is soured on life and has nothing good to say about anything or anyone. The lens of both of these positions will either raise faith or give in to fear. What we see tends to become our reality. We can affect our reality by the seat we choose. You may want to change seats after reading this chapter.

One medical school reported that at least 50 percent of medical students complained of symptoms of the diseases they were studying. The principle of magnification is very real. Whatever we continue to view brings us into the picture.

Jesus said, "I say to you that everyone who looks at a woman with lust for her has *already committed adultery with her in his heart*" (Matthew 5:28). Jesus is showing how powerful imagination really is. If you should lust (more than a casual look, to fix on to) for her, it becomes a reality though the act of adultery was not carried through. Because the power of imagination is so real, the opposite could be used for good. Instead of a vain imagination, we could develop a godly imagination. Consider imagining the power of God to heal and raise the dead or to be translated across the planet like Phillip was. If the imagination of adultery is powerful, then the imagination to see the Kingdom of God manifested is also very real.

> *And He took him outside and said, "Now look toward the heavens, and count the stars, if you are able to count them." And He said to him, "So shall your descendants be"* (Genesis 15:5).

God took Abram outside his tent so he could see further than himself. He wanted him to have a picture to wrap his thinking around. Abram heard the promise of a son and tried to make it happen through using his maid as a surrogate. God reminded him that this was not the promised seed, but the one coming from him and Sarah was. Abram could now see that the promise was far greater than having a son; it was about birthing a nation. Once he could see the stars as a picture of what a seed could produce, he then believed in the Lord and God reckoned it to him as righteousness.

Perhaps you have a small seed of a picture on the inside of you but can't quite bring it to fulfillment. Ask the Lord to let you see what it would look like. You can walk out something that has been pictured on the inside. Nothing is impossible where there is unity of purpose and unity of language with a vision.

God saw the intent of the hearts of those wanting to build a city with a tower to make a name for themselves. God saw that nothing that they had purposed or imagined would be withheld from them (see Genesis 11:6). In order to stop the work on the tower of Babel, God changed their languages, and today we see the result of it. When people are joined to a task and they can all picture the result, nothing is impossible.

WRITE THE VISION

In Habakkuk 1, the prophet says the burden of the Lord is upon him. In Habakkuk 2, God tells him to write the vision and make it plain so that those who read it can run. Many of us look for the vision first to find motivation for what we are to do. The Holy Spirit will first bring a burden or a sense of passion. The weightiness of that burden will allow you to begin to see. We receive burdens through praying, and in those times of deep interaction with the Spirit, He transfers a burden to us. It's easier to see something that you are moved about than to try to envision what it is.

Jesus saw the large crowd following and He began teaching them (see Mark 6:34–37). Due to the late hour the disciples suggested to Jesus that He should send them away so they could find food. Jesus told the disciples to feed them. The miracle was there, they just didn't have the vision for what was to happen. Jesus was moved with compassion on the multitude because they were like sheep without a shepherd. Compassion is a deep, innermost burden that grips to the point of causing action. Jesus was *moved* with this burden. None of the disciples seemed to be touched by what they saw, and they were ready to let them go. Vision without burden rarely gets any traction. Jesus just asked for what was available; He took what He had and blessed it and broke it, not waiting for it to multiply. The multiplying took place as they gave what they had away.

While ministering in Cuba many years ago we were faced with something similar although not to the magnitude here. The people were very poor and there was rationing on the basics, even rice and beans. Under communist rule, the state owns everything and they decide what you will be allowed to own and even to eat. We were scheduled to go to the other end of the island to visit a pastor and help in any way we could. We were able to buy a few pounds of rice and beans and a live chicken at a government store that took dollars. We made the rough ride and we took turns holding the live chicken. There was supposed to be a family of six and our team of four. The home was on the edge of the jungle. While the pastor and his family prepared the meal, people began coming out of the jungle. They were friends and people of the church the pastor led, and soon the dinner invitation grew to 45. I told our host that it would be okay for us to do without dinner as we could wait until we returned to the hotel. The host replied, "Oh no, you must eat first." The room that housed the table and chairs was near the hot plate that was used for cooking. We blessed the food and ate until we were full. We moved aside for the next group to be seated. I stood next to the pots that held the rice and beans mixed with chicken. Every time they dipped the spoon in to take out food I could not see that anything changed. The amount stayed the same until the last group was seated and the sound of an empty pot being scraped with the spoon could be heard. There is no way in the natural that a scrawny chicken and a few pounds of rice and beans could have fed such a crowd. I told the pastor I was amazed; he replied, "Why?" He said, "This is the way we have to live. When we pray, we believe He is the Bread of Life."

THINGS THAT KILL VISION

1. **Lack of communication:** Those who carry vision must express it to others. Those they want to enlist help from must be able to see the finished product. The leaders who can articulate the path and the benefits of the project will win over hearts to follow.

2. **Lack of delegation:** The next step of implementation is to let others share in the imagining along with you. They will bring pieces to the mix that you never thought of. It takes a secure individual to allow the project to move forward when others begin to share what you carried as an infant seed. There may be times when the secondary leader may change a number of times to allow each particular phase to move forward. Not every leader carries what is needed all the time. The primary leader who began the articulation of the dream continues to put forth approval and tweaking when necessary.

3. **Lack of participation:** At this level there will again need to be a releasing of others to join the project. There will need to be an articulation as new participants join your vision. It is somewhat more difficult to motivate the new participants because some of the work at this stage is not as exciting. The originator of the vision must then give honor where honor is due and speak of the benefits of seeing the project all the way to the end.

4. **Lack of discipline:** When all the newness and excitement of the vision has begun to wane, discipline will need to be reinforced. When someone has unrealistic expectations of the time it will take, they may lose focus or attention to the details. All projects or visions will have resistance. Nehemiah took on the enormity of rebuilding the walls of Jerusalem, but there were obstacles to overcome. Nehemiah had to deal with those who were trying to pull him off the wall for a debate about the vision of rebuilding the walls. Nehemiah showed a strong sense of discipline by continually answering them by saying, "The work is so great I cannot come down from the wall and stop the work." The discipline of focus is crucial. The longer a vision takes to complete, the greater the need for discipline is.

The Lord will give you the ability to see the work of your hands through to completion. If the vision tarries, wait for it.

Chapter 12

BRINGING OUT
THE BEST IN YOU

"Practice makes perfect"—that was the mantra that was drilled into our heads every day. Playing tennis at a competitive level in high school was one of the few things I looked forward to on a daily basis at that time. Our coach had played at that level in his younger days and still competed. He didn't have much patience for players who just wanted the exercise. He was a die-hard tennis player. One day at practice when I was warming up with him, he said, "Kirkwood, the way you warm up is the way you will play today; now get your head into today." I admitted that I had other things on my mind at the time, like mid-term exams. He proceeded to take his lecture to the next level and brought the whole team in closer for his philosophy of life and everything it touches. He said, *"Practice makes perfect only when you practice perfectly."* I got the message clearly, and that was that *you groove into habits unconsciously and you deal with things from those habitual memories.* You may not know why you reacted angrily when a particular subject came up in trivial conversation. It was because you practiced a way of thinking that was now part of the auto-response mechanism. My coach finished up with his motivation for being tough with us: "I want to bring out the best of who you are, which is the real you; you have to decide if you want that person to emerge or not." He certainly got my attention, but I was not sure who the real me was. I thought I knew, but after his little philosophy lesson, it made me wonder. One day while in tournament play, I was upset with myself for letting a player beat me who I knew shouldn't have. My coach came over to me, and I thought I was going to get another lecture about team responsibility, but instead he smiled and put his arm around me and said, "You are better that that; don't let today define who you really are." It made me want to play harder and smarter because I was better than yesterday had shown.

Today the battle is not on the tennis court, but the battle is in my thinking. I am taking thoughts captive as if they were my opponents. I try to warm up for the day by meditating on the goodness of God and replaying in my thinking all the wonderful things I get to enjoy because Jesus championed my cause. Practicing right thinking is valuable when we practice thinking perfectly by letting it be about Him.

> *Now the Lord is the Spirit, and where the Spirit of the Lord is, there is liberty. But we all, with unveiled face, beholding as in a mirror the glory of the Lord, are being transformed into the same image from glory to glory, just as from the Lord, the Spirit* (2 Corinthians 3:17–18).

The exhortation here is exciting. We become what we behold. Beholding something implies that we are holding something valuable close for inspection and what we are beholding carries a profound effect upon us. Liberty in this context means to be unrestrained, saying, "Where the Holy Spirit is allowed to be Lord, we are not held back—the sky or our imagination is the only limit." When the Holy Spirit is in charge He brings out the best in us. The best means the ultimate that we were created to be. In the earlier chapters, I brought into the discussion how God wrote a book about our possibilities. I would say that is our best—the Holy Spirit leading and coaching us based upon what has been written. I think that book has more about our nature and character than the career choice we make. God loves us no matter what our career, but integrity and purity are the values He most wants to see us practice perfectly. The primary message from this passage is transformation. He wants to give us a picture or image of our best through His eyes so we will be changed from one level of glory to the next. Glory is God's covering; it's the filter through which He wants us to view Him and the world.

EYES OF GLORY

Genesis 2:25 describes Adam and Eve right after God had finished creating Eve—they were both naked and not ashamed. They were not aware of what shame was. There was no need for that thought to be defined because it did not exist. Many believe—and I agree with this—that the glory of God covered them, and when Adam would look at Eve he looked through the filter of the glory and vice versa. Everything looks better when it is viewed through the eyes of glory. *There are no offences in glory.* After Eve accepted the lie of the serpent, the glory departed. Adam and Eve saw one another through the eyes of knowledge of good and evil. Their spirits lost the dominance of communing with God easily, and now their minds stepped in and took the lead. *Life looked different because they lost the eyes of glory, and shame was now defined as the absence of God's glory.*

"Set your mind on the things above, not on the things that are on earth. For you have died and your life is hidden with Christ in God. When Christ, who is our life, is revealed, then you also will be revealed with Him in glory" (Colossians 3:2-4). To bring out the best in us we are told to set or fix a point like on a compass and keep sight of that fixed point and not deviate from our course, letting that set point be the guiding force in our life. In line with this thinking, in order to bring out our greatness we need to be around others who are stronger and fixed upon the things of God. In tennis play it was often said, "If you want to improve your game, you should play others who are stronger than you, which will up your game to a higher level." Our social environment can affect our mind spiritually. Lot did not start out thinking like a permanent resident of Sodom. The Bible describes Lot as one whose soul/mind was vexed daily. Let other strong believers challenge you to bring out the real inner person because you are better than that.

"Do not lie to one another, since you laid aside the old self with its evil practices, and have put on the new self who is being renewed to a *true knowledge according to the image of the One who created him*" (Col. 3:9–10). The principle of life is that something has to be fed to live and what is starved dies. In this case the old man, who represents the carnal opposition to

God's best for us, dies when we no longer feed it with excuses for sin. The new man represents the target image of Christ. That is the fixed compass point we are to fix our gaze upon. The word for "old" here is *palaios,* meaning "worn out, no longer pliable to be stretched." In essence, the old person of the heart cannot grow and resists the change that the new man desires. Second Corinthians 5:17 says, "Therefore if anyone is in Christ, he is a new creature; the old things passed away; behold, new things have come." The theme continues on to instruct us that our best only comes through when we become a creation—a creation that was destined for eternal death and now has been transformed into a new species destined for eternal life. The cocoon of the old passes away and is no longer part of our new best. The most miserable place to be is desiring to be a new creation and attempting to drag along the old man; he can't make the trip to the new and improved you. Remember the verse in Second Corinthians 4:16, "Therefore we do not lose heart, but though our outer man is decaying, yet our inner man is being renewed day by day." The outward man is daily collecting mileage for expiration, but the new you is getting a daily make over.

STANDING OUT IN ADVERSITY

But the Lord said to Samuel, "Do not look at his appearance or at the height of his stature, because I have rejected him; for God sees not as man sees, for man looks at the outward appearance, but the Lord looks at the heart" (1 Samuel 16:7).

God sent the prophet Samuel to the family of Jesse to anoint and set in place the next king. When Samuel arrived all the sons of Jesse were made to pass by Samuel. When he saw Eliab, he said, "Surely the Lord's anointed is standing here." Samuel was ready to anoint this one because he looked kingly. He looked a lot like Saul, and through comparison he looked like he could replace Saul. God made His choice not based upon the outward; He looked at the heart. By this time, Saul had disobeyed God and reasoned away his disobedience, thinking that God would approve based on his analysis, but God had rejected him. After Samuel had gone through all the sons who were before him, he asked if this were all his sons. Jesse said, "There is one out tending the sheep, but he is only a youngster."

Samuel said, "We will not sit down until you bring him." When David came to them he was different from his brothers. He was smaller and ruddy in complexion, yet God chose him because of his heart toward God. Samuel anointed David in front of his brothers, and the Spirit of the Lord came upon David from that day forward. David spent much of his time playing music and musing about God, and because his heart was fixed on things above, his heart found a place before God. Though David had been anointed king, not much had changed in his life. The day would come when God would bring out this young man and show Himself mighty through this lad.

David was sent by his father to take some food to his older brothers, who were facing the Philistines in Saul's army, and bring back any news. David heard the taunts of Goliath, and no one seemed to be motivated to respond. David took the challenge and had to get past his brothers' insults. He finally made his way up to Saul, who tried to outfit him with armor that didn't fit. After all, David had never worn armor before or found himself facing a human opponent, but the Spirit of

God was moving upon and through him. When Goliath had fallen and the Philistines started to run, things would never be the same. Israel had found a champion who showed leadership and who would prove to be a man after God's own heart. The adversity had proven to be his coming-out party. Everyone knew him now. He was no longer the little shepherd boy but was now the giant killer.

Adversity challenges are not set in our path for failure but to bring out the best in us. Without problems and crises, we would not have many of the inventions and appliances we take for granted today. Henry Ford developed the assembly line due to the demand for military hardware because of World War II. God prepares people in hard times to develop breakthrough strategies that will last a lifetime. Problems don't define who we are, but our reaction to them does. Faith is developed out of times of difficulty that stretch us to our limits. We find in times of testing that we are more capable than we knew, because the times that try men's souls are the times that raise them to the top. In times of peace we learn very little, though that is what we want to achieve. The pioneer spirit in many caused new lands to be discovered. Some were discontent to live out their lives as settlers and became intrigued by what was on the other side of the world. Today, travel is accepted as an easy fact. There are those who want to be the best at what they do so they excel beyond the status quo.

IN LOVE OR IN FEAR

By this, love is perfected with us, so that we may have confidence in the day of judgment; because as He is, so also are we in this world (1 John 4:17).

For love to be perfected in us, we need occasions when love is challenged. The opposite of love is fear; so fear is our opponent that brings out the best in us. Fear puts up a fight that love can conquer, and each time love wins we become more in love than in fear. *Fear has torment and love has peace; the two cannot coexist.* Some of the strongest ministries dealing with witchcraft-type fear were those who had experienced the torment stemming from fear. It was being challenged with this stronghold that brought out the deliverer in them. Many times the area that's the weakest becomes the strongest. The bone that is broken grows back stronger than before. The Holy Spirit is all about bringing out the inner strength of what we are called to be. *The very thing you are dealing with right now is the stepping stone perfecting love in you for the future.* Remember, love is not a gushy feeling of sentiment; it is the power to cast out fear. John reminds us in this passage that we are right now as Jesus is right now. He sees Himself in us, so love will be perfected. Love will mature to the point that love will be the choice over being offended. The next time you feel you are being offended, just think, *I am going to choose love here and now because as Jesus is right at this moment so am I. Jesus is not offended, so I am not offended. I forgive them just as Jesus forgives them.* As He is, so are we in this present world. By this we know that love has reached a level of perfection in us.

PULLING GREATNESS OUT OF YOU

Don was a good player on our tennis team, but it seemed the coach was personally picking on him. He would be critiqued over minor things, and looking on as a bystander I could see where Don felt he was being singled out. I noticed the more he was pushed by the coach, the better Don played under pressure. When asked about his tough stance with Don, the coach said, "I see something in him that he doesn't see for himself, and if he can't see what he could be, he will settle for mediocrity. He has what it takes to be great, but greatness doesn't just emerge without bringing it to the surface." Many die with greatness in them but never had it pulled from them to make a difference in the world. Though many of the lessons centered on tennis, they were applied in life skills. There is no Bible story that better fits this scenario of greatness being brought out of another than the history of Elijah and Elisha. The story begins with God telling Elijah to anoint Elisha to take his place (see 1 Kings 19:19).

The relationship began with Elijah just pitching his coat over Elisha, saying, "Follow me." Elisha explained to him that he was busy at the moment taking care of the family farm. Maybe he was thinking that Elijah would understand, seeing all the plowing as he walked up. Elisha was trying to make a deal about the timing and said, "Okay, I will come, but first I need to kiss my parents goodbye, and then I am tracking with you." That was a cultural way of saying, "When my parents die and I have no responsibilities, I will come."

Elijah said (my paraphrase), "Then what am I doing taking time with you?" Someone who has yet to understand what the end game is will be somewhat reluctant to lay everything down and follow. He had a word from God, so he knew this mentorship had to be intentional. Elisha served Elijah for about ten years, or the span from First Kings 19 to Second Kings 2. During that time, Elisha saw some powerful miracles and life became quite different from the farm life he was found in. God saw something in Elisha that would take time to bring to the level of greatness he was called to. The time came when Elijah asked his spiritual son, "What do you want me to do for you?" The point I want to make here is that *without seeing what our best looks like or could be, we won't know what to ask for.* Elisha had ten years of modeling what his life could be. He didn't just ask for Elijah's mantle/ministry; Elisha asked for a double portion of his spirit. This was the term used by a firstborn son who had a right to the double portion as the executor of the family estate. The firstborn would then in turn distribute the wealth to the rest of the family. It appeared Elisha was beginning to understand that all of this was for the purpose of serving his nation.

Being our best is not for trophies or bragging rights but for the purpose of serving. Elijah admitted it would not be easy for Elisha to have what he was asking for, but if he saw him being taken up, it would be as he asked. In Second Kings 2, you will find Elijah testing Elisha three times by suggesting Elisha wait at a particular place until he returned. Elisha answered each time, "As the Lord lives and your soul lives I will not leave you." So it was on the day of Elijah's spectacular departure, Elisha saw the glory of God and took the mantle that fell from Elisha.

I will give this conjecture here—possibly Elisha could have received Elijah's mantle by simply being around him, but the "double portion" part was more difficult; even Elijah said it was difficult. I suggest that the second portion came by encountering the glory that Elijah was caught up in. Some things we get through teaching, while the deep things come through encountering; or we could say some things are taught, others are caught. Elisha had to catch what fell from Elijah. No one really knows how things will manifest unless they sign on for the full ride. The best is yet to come, and the best of you is yet to come forth. Though some of the tutors we are assigned are not the easiest to learn from, they might just be the ones God uses to pull greatness out of you. "But we have this treasure in earthen vessels, so that the surpassing greatness of the power will be of God and not from ourselves" (2 Corinthians 4:7). The power of the Spirit is what ultimately is at work to bring forth all that has been written about you.

Chapter 13

DEVELOPING THE SEER IN YOU

Having right thinking is crucial to being one who sees from God's perspective. As one thinks, so will he see based on how he thinks. Two people looking at the same picture or scene will report what they see driven by what is most dominant in their thinking. For example, my wife Diane and I were watching a movie and the typical commercial came on. The advertisement was focusing on a new kitchen-cleaning product. The scene showed two small boys getting Mom's baking flour and with the help of a couple of water guns, they looked to be having a good time—until Mom walked in. The lady of the house didn't panic, but took the premier cleaning product and quickly cleaned up the mess, showing how easy it was to clean with the new product.

I said, "Man, that looks like something my brother and I would have gotten into."

Diane said, "Where was the mother who left them unsupervised? And there is no way anyone is going to get all that flour dust cleaned up."

Diane, being very organized and tidy, saw the commercial through her thinking. I was viewing the advertisement through my filter and background. Interestingly enough, neither one of us paid attention to the product being pitched. So we can see how thinking shapes our view of things both tangible and intangible. Experience plays a role in developing thoughts that connect with what is observed. When I saw the two boys mixing it up it took me back to some good times I had with my friends. Diane, in her experience as a mother, was concerned about keeping a clean and orderly home. This is why the renewing of our minds is necessary to be able to see through God's perspective. People tend to pray the way they think about a particular subject. If their mind has yet to be renewed and see through biblical compliance, they may be praying their will or perspective being done instead of God's plan enacted. Faith is not released through what we think about something, but faith is powerful when coupled with the Scripture and what God says.

> *I would have despaired unless I had believed that I would see the goodness of the Lord in the land of the living* (Psalm 27:13).

Failure to see correctly could be the difference between receiving and feeling overlooked. The psalmist makes the point, "If I had not believed I would see God's goodness, I would have lost all sense of hope and courage." Failure to see what God is doing could cause one to misunderstand and wrongly think that God is saying *no* when in reality things have to be removed so what you believe to see can come. Circumstances are not always the best indicator of progress in regard to your prayer being answered. Ask the Holy Spirit to show you what the finished result looks like. In the meantime, don't measure what you see as the final answer. Someone asked a famous sculptor how he came up with his large sculptures. He said, *"I have a picture in my mind of what I want the project to look like, and I begin chiseling away everything that doesn't look like what I am seeing."* When standing for something you are seeing, don't get distracted by the parts that don't resemble what you are looking for. Keep your focus upon the prize of the finished work.

There is a fable of a king whose son was born deformed and hunched over to the point that he could not straighten up. He asked his father if he would commission a statue of himself standing upright for his sixteenth birthday. His father questioned him to see if he was sure because it seemed a cruel thing to do. The son assured the king that this was his desire. The day it was finished the king asked his son, "Where should we display the statue?" His son requested for it to be set up outside his bedroom window. Every morning the young boy would position himself in a way that he could see the life-sized statue of himself. On his twenty-first birthday, the king's son shocked everyone by walking into the dining room upright. His father asked, "How did this happen?"

His son replied, "One day at a time, I could see what I am supposed to be." Getting free from stagnant thinking that keeps one bent over, never being able to look up, is a huge accomplishment.

WHAT DO YOU SEE?

Ezekiel 37 is a favorite account of seeing the way God wants us to see. Ezekiel was having a vision of the condition of Israel at that time. He was taken to a valley and there were bleached, dry bones. None of the bones were connected and all were scattered. God asked the question of Ezekiel, "Can these bones live?"

I wonder, why the question? Just tell him what you want him to do. I believe God wants to partner with us in such a way that He shares with us the reality of what we are seeing. Ezekiel answered, "Only You know, God." Ezekiel was instructed to prophesy over the bones. If Ezekiel had not had the sight to see what God wanted him to see, he could have prophesied against the bones. The bones began to move together. Bones that were on the other side of the valley found their proper place and fit—bones flying all around because he could see the possibility in the face of destruction. He prophesied to the wind, and breath was restored and they stood up as an army.

HOW DO YOU SEE YOURSELF?

A renewed mind is renewed spiritual eyes that will look through heart eyes of faith. *Renewed* means to be refreshed or resuscitated. I picture the wind of the Spirit breathing into me and bringing me back from the dead life to a life alive in Him.

"For indeed we have had good news preached to us, just as they also; but the word they heard did not profit them, because it was not united by faith in those who heard" (Hebrews 4:2). The writer was referring to the Hebrews wandering in the wilderness for 40 years, who heard the report of God's promises.

They heard good news but did not apply faith to what they heard, and as a result they did not enter the place of rest that had been promised 430 years previously to Abraham. The thinking of the Hebrews by this time was tied to their experience living in Egypt. When the opportunity arose for them to see their future and destiny finally fulfilled, they chose not to enter in. Their thinking had become adapted to being nomads. When a land filled with good things was made available, they could not see themselves living beyond where they were at the present.

There is a seer in all of us if we apply faith to the promise and claim it to be ours. The thinking of an orphan will say, "This is too good to be true." The thinking of a seer will say like Caleb did when his time of possession came around, "This is my mountain, and I am just as strong today as when God promised it to me" (see Joshua 14:6–12). Joshua and Caleb were the only two spies God allowed to enter into their inheritance of the land of Canaan. They were the only two who reported what they saw mixed with faith. Those who did not enter the land of promise carried the same promise that God spoke to all the twelve tribes. Yet they died with a promise; they did not die *in the promise.*

I have conducted many funeral services for members of my congregation of all ages. On a number of occasions, I would have this question posed to me while standing over the casket of a loved one: "They had many prophetic words that were unfulfilled; how can they die and not see the fulfillment of these promises?" The only answer is the one I read above in Hebrews. At some point, seeing something possible must be met with movement of faith toward the vision. There are different reasons for not seeing their promise through to the end.

Hebrews 11:13–16 gives comfort by revealing that though there are those who died in faith, they saw the promise distantly and were seeking it, and they had the testimony that they pleased God. Even though they didn't enter into what they believed for, God was pleased that they lived as though they had received. I think God delights in the process we go through to get to the point of fulfillment, because in the journey we gain a closer relationship to God.

TRAINING MY THOUGHTS

For who among men knows the thoughts of a man except the spirit of the man which is in him? Even so the thoughts of God no one knows except the Spirit of God. **Now we have received, not the spirit of the world,** *but the Spirit who is from God, so that we may know the things freely given to us by God* (1 Corinthians 2:11–12).

To train our thinking to conform to the imagination of God, we need to know that it will take more than willpower to accomplish this new pattern of thinking. We really don't know our self, but our spirit knows us. It takes the Holy Spirit working in our spirit to begin this reformation through conviction of sin and establishing a pure heart. To truly know God it takes the Holy Spirit to show the Father's heart. Paul emphasizes that we did not receive the spirit of the world. The spirit of the world is not received like we receive the Holy Spirit. The spirit of the world is learned behavior. It is modeled through Hollywood actors and through types of idolatry that call evil good and good evil. When our thoughts accept this type of thinking we have a "triad spirit." The thinking in this present system has attempted to do away with absolutes. The prevailing thought in New Age thinking is that whatever brings you peace is an acceptable practice. This spirit is now in conflict with the Spirit of God, who has laid down absolutes to give freedom from the adversary, the devil, who goes about like a lion looking for prey. The prey is anyone who accepts the spirit of the world.

The third part of this triad conflict is our own spirit—the part of us that God breathed into us to know Him and have a hunger to search for God. The spirit of the world wants to change the real you and who you were meant to be by oppressing the hunger to know God by grieving your spirit through countless times overriding your conscience. This overriding begins to erode the absolutes that the Holy Spirit placed inside you to discern the danger of the enemy of your soul/thinking. On the contrary, when you recognize the enemy wants to place a thought that does not line up with who you know God to be and you immediately reject that thought, you have won the round. In the same way this spirit of the world was acquired—through observing the world system and giving acquiescence—we can learn new ways of the culture of the Kingdom of God.

Anything magnified is easier to see. In the same respect, what we magnify takes the biggest picture frame of the mind and will take up the space. A few years ago while asking the Lord for a solution to a problem, I heard Him say in the quietness of my spirit, "To shrink the problem you must magnify the solution." It made perfect sense to me because I had been doing the opposite. I was magnifying the problem, telling everyone who would ask how I was doing. Psalm 34:3 came to mind while tossing around that thought in my head,

"Oh magnify the Lord with me, and let us exalt His name together." I realized I was either making the problem bigger than God or I was going to magnify God bigger than the problem. Paul said that what we yield the members of our body to, we are enslaved by. So I decided to change my thinking, and with every issue that arose, I would talk about all the times the Lord had come through for my family and me. I was not going to allow the spirit of the world to jump in and start complaining. Complaining is a way of saying "God, You have not taken very good care of me." Magnifying God is training our thoughts to hear the thoughts the Lord has over us. Remember Jeremiah 29:11 that says *He has thoughts that He thinks toward us to give us a hope and future.* Magnifying the Lord through worship and thanksgiving allows you to hear the thoughts He has toward you more clearly. The triad conflict falls away, and now the only two left are the Spirit of God and our spirit, which gives us the mind of Christ.

DOESN'T COMPUTE

While having breakfast one morning in Seoul, South Korea, I noticed a couple on the other side of this large dining room. Immediately I felt the impression from the Lord that He had something to say to them. My mind quickly joined the conversation, reminding me that they probably did not speak English. My heart reminded me that the Holy Spirit knew that before I was prompted to speak to them. I thought, *This doesn't compute, because we are not in church where I usually get this type of urging by the Holy Spirit.* I thought a compromise might work, thinking to myself, *Well, if they are still there when I finish eating I will mosey on over there.* I felt the strong sense that if I didn't go immediately, I would be disobedient to the Holy Spirit and I would not have favor for ministering in the conference that was beginning later that morning. I thought, *Well, if they don't speak English—because we are, after all, in an international hotel—then I am off the hook.* I slowly made my way up to the table and said, "Excuse me."

They answered, "Yes?"

Now I knew they spoke English, but I noticed the wife seemed to be crying. I said, "I have a message from our Father, and he sent me to tell you it's okay for you to lay down your schedule for the next three months and have time with Him; after that time of healing and rest the anointing will be greater than what you have known in the past."

I quickly turned and left to go back to my table, and I finished my breakfast and left for the conference. I couldn't get away from what had happened because it just didn't make rational sense to do this in a strange place. At least I felt better for having obeyed, and I would never see those people again, who probably thought I was crazy anyway. The next morning I was at the same table enjoying a quiet breakfast before the busy schedule of the day began. Ten minutes into the breakfast, the same couple walked up to me and said, "May we join you?"

I said, "Yes, of course."

We introduced ourselves to one another, only to find out they were on staff at a well-known ministry in the U.S. He said, "When you came up to our table, we were just having a discussion about how exhausted we were, and my wife was in tears because we could not see how we could take any time off, when out of nowhere a complete stranger said, 'God wants you to take three months off.' We both were just praising the Lord together for loving us so much that you would speak to us unexpectedly."

Many times, thoughts of the Lord will not make sense because we look for the whole picture when all we know is a small part. Every time we give in to thoughts of the Lord, it becomes easier to know His voice.

MY THOUGHTS ARE NOT YOURS

> *"For My thoughts are not your thoughts, nor are your ways My ways," declares the Lord. "For as the heavens are higher than the earth, so are My ways higher than your ways and My thoughts than your thoughts"* (Isaiah 55:8–9).

In training our thoughts to be tuned to the seer in us, we must realize that not every thought that passes through the processing of the mind is a thought initiated by the Holy Spirit. As we have mentioned in earlier chapters, we are to test the spirits to see whether they are of God. There are attributes that are characteristic of God. We know that God will not violate or overrule His own Word of Truth. Romans 12:6 explains this: "Since we have gifts that differ according to the grace given to us, each of us is to exercise them accordingly: if prophecy, *according to the proportion of his faith*." Notice that prophecy is released at the level of our faith. Boldness is not faith. One can be bold through their personality and not have faith. We test the thoughts of prophecy through the filter of our faith. "So then faith comes from hearing, and hearing by the word of Christ" (Romans 10:17). One thing affects the other. Our spiritual level of hearing is developed through the deposit of the Word of God inside of us. Putting all into a nice package, we would say we can judge our thoughts through the Word of God, and to the level we have faith, we can use those thoughts given to us by the Holy Spirit to build up others.

In order to prophesy effectively, we should not attempt to do so out of soulish boldness, which could be viewed as pride or arrogance, but instead out of the deposit of the word you received through faith. That deposit will only continue to grow when submitting to the Holy Spirit, who is the Spirit of Truth. Psalm 119:11 says, "Your word I have treasured in my heart, that I may not sin against You." Again, when the word is deposited within our heart we are not searching for words to prophesy because the word is already in your heart, waiting for faith to release it into the hearing of another. *It's out of the abundance of the heart that the mouth speaks.* When the heart is filled with God's thoughts through His Word, it easily flows out very naturally. What will seem natural to you will become supernatural to someone else.

I should insert here, because I have seen this happen—don't try to copy another person's personality or style of delivery. Shouting or saying "Thus saith the Lord" doesn't make the word any more powerful or authentic. It will come out of your spirit and be delivered through your soul, which is your personality and intellect. In fact, if our style of delivery is over the top and theatrical it becomes more about the messenger than the message. Then the purpose of giving the message for edification, exhortation, and comfort is lost in the delivery and the message is diluted.

The first time I gave a word publicly in an open congregation (at 19 years old) I was terrified. I had a million things running through my mind all at the same time, it seemed, and most of them were fear related, which is based in self. Most of what I felt was fear of rejection, fear of saying something wrong or being publicly humiliated and embarrassing my family. I had choked back the prompting to go for it a couple of weeks prior. The day arrived when it happened again; the prompting of the Lord was persistent. I opened my mouth, thinking that there would be awesome revelation flowing out like a smooth, gentle river. Instead, I said, "God is good," and not another word came out of my mouth. The time delay seemed like minutes but was probably two seconds before I realized that was all that was in me. I went home, fell across my bed, and repented for missing it. I felt somewhat embarrassed, like a child learning to ride a bike without training wheels; *I skinned my knees pretty good,* I thought.

After a time, when my own thoughts of self-pity ran out, I heard in my spirit the sweetest voice, like a father picking up his son from a fall off his bike. This is what I heard: "I gave you just enough to see what you would do with it, and to see if you would know when to stop when I stopped speaking through you."

I said, "But Lord, one word and it wasn't deep at all."

The answer was quick and to the point. "Doesn't My Word say I am good?" The lesson I learned that day was not to despise small beginnings and not to judge spiritual things with natural instincts.

SEPARATING SOUL AND SPIRIT

For the word of God is living and powerful, and sharper than any two-edged sword, piercing even to the division of soul and spirit, and of joints and *marrow, and is a **discerner of the thoughts and intents of the heart*** (Hebrews 4:12 NKJV).

There are two main points that we should extract for the purpose of developing the seer in all of us. Number one—we should never doubt the life of the Word of God. It is not just random vocabulary, but the Word is living to the point of being creative. When you are using the Word in delivering a message it becomes alive and is transformative. I believe it is a stronger message when it is Word-oriented and not just story-telling. Is the Word at the center of what you are saying? If the Word is not woven into the word directly there could be more soul and less spirit in the message. Second, the Word makes a distinction between soul and spirit. Soul (*psuche*) is the intellectual part of us that seeks relevancy and sensibility, which is temporary. Our spirit (*pneuma*) is the part that was breathed into us and is eternal. The spirit part of us doesn't need a logical track to run on but only a Word track to move on. The Holy Spirit of God quickens our spirit when there is the Word of God involved. The Word helps discern the thoughts and intents of the heart. For instance, we can find ways to justify an action using our soul. But when the Word becomes the judge in the matter, our spirit comes into agreement and we feel either the conviction of conscience or we experience a surge of faith.

THE LAST ADAM

Now look in First Corinthians 15:45: "So also it is written [quoting the Old Testament], 'The first man, Adam, became a living soul.' The last Adam became a life-giving spirit." Let's take a close look at the distinction. *The first Adam became a living soul.* The first Adam God created out of the dust was a living being (speaking spirit). The second Adam is the Son of the Living God—Jesus. Jesus was the second Adam and the last Adam. *The last Adam became a life-giving spirit.* The first Adam was a speaking spirit, but the last Adam became a life-giving spirit. The first Adam failed in the Garden of Eden (translated, "place of His presence"), and the second Adam, Jesus, overcame in the Garden of Gethsemane and gave His life as a ransom. The first Adam failed due to disobedience; the second Adam won victory through His obedience.

The Adam who failed could only speak in terms of being like God, and he lost his place of glory. The Son of the Living God came to restore the relationship between God and humankind in such a way that the *last Adam became a life-giving spirit.* The Bible says in First John 5:16 that if you see someone sinning, a sin that's not unto death, pray that the person would have life. In other words, the last Adam, the life-giving Spirit, is now giving to us the Spirit of life to speak life over those who are stumbling through life. The Bible says the power of life and death is in the tongue (see Proverbs 18:21). We are a speaking spirit with power to choose life! When we choose to speak cursing over people, we are falling back into the first Adam thinking. But as a son, you choose life because life speaks as the Son of the Living God. You are a life-giving spirit now operating in glory and being revealed in glory.

BLESSING VERSUS CURSING

Finally, all of you be of one mind, having compassion for one another; love as brothers, be tenderhearted, be courteous; not returning evil for evil or reviling for reviling, but on the contrary blessing, knowing that you were called to this, that you may inherit a blessing (1 Peter 3:8–9 NKJV).

The power that is in blessing is phenomenal. The word for blessing here is *eulogeo,* from which we get our English word *eulogy. Eulogeo* means to speak well of. My definition of *blessing* is to speak God's intentions over someone or something. Instead of reporting how bad someone is, why not declare over them that they are the creation of God created for good works? It may appear to be the opposite of the facts, but blessing is prophetic. We are calling things into their intended place. The above verse states that when we choose to bless, we are then in a position to inherit a blessing. The Bible teaches that what we have done to others is the same as if we had done it to Jesus.

Cursing is placing someone or something in a lower position than what God intended. The Word of God is a discerner of the thoughts and intentions of the heart, so we should speak His intentions over everything. When we agree with God He will even make our enemies to be at peace with us. God promised Abraham a son, and by all natural observance of him and his wife Sarah it seemed impossible. Abraham was told to consider the things that are not as though they were done (see Romans 4:17). Blessing is prophetic in the same way—we look past the natural circumstances and speak the thoughts of God. Jesus said we were to bless those who curse us (see Luke 6:28). The idea goes against thoughts of our soul. The first Adam wants to defend his rights; the last Adam, the life-giving Spirit, wants to come in the opposite spirit and bless. To develop the seer in us, we must be conformed to the image of the last Adam, the one who blesses. The accuser in Revelation 12:10 we could say is the curser because he is accursed, and he wants us to agree with him and have thoughts about others so we can curse them.

Here is a testimony from a lady who was listening to the CD series I taught on the power of blessing. She was an office manager of a small company. The employees were her friends, so they would confide in her with their feelings about various things. Over a period of time, complaining crept into the office and she found herself agreeing with them. She began voicing her disproval of the boss and his decisions on everything. She noticed that the boss began to be more distant from her and that encouraged more cursing by her and the office staff. Things ramped up to the point where she was fairly sure she was going to be fired from her job. A friend gave her the series on blessing and the more she listened, the more she could identify herself as a curser. She decided she was going to try what she had learned.

Monday morning she opened the office early and went from room to room speaking God's intentions for the business and for the other employees. She would not accept the usual complaining that brought the agreement of cursing in the beginning. She continued to bless her boss by giving thanks for the opportunity to make a good living. She blessed his family, that they would see the goodness of the Lord in everything their hands touched. By the end of the week her boss called her into his office. She thought she was going to be let go right then by the look on his face. She realized that she probably deserved it too, for being party to all the strife in the office. He began by saying, "I have not been nice to you, and I am sorry for that. I want to make it up to you by giving you the raise you deserve retroactive as of three months ago." She came out of his office dumbfounded. She realized that blessing really turns things in your favor when you choose to see things from God's point of view.

Let me conclude with this thought. Revelation 19:10 says, "The testimony of Jesus is the spirit of prophecy." Carrying thoughts of blessing will ensure that speaking blessing to others is like the spirit of prophecy that testifies of Jesus. As we bless others we are sharing the prophetic heart of Christ, and it brings back blessing upon us.

Lord, I pray that those who have read this book would be a depository of Your thoughts and intents. May each know the thoughts that You have for them and carry those thoughts into discerning Your heart for their hope and future. I ask that each one will be quickened by the Holy Spirit to speak under the influence of Your love for the Body of Christ, and we would always represent You on earth as You really are in heaven. Amen!

OTHER BOOKS BY KERRY KIRKWOOD

The Power of Blessing

The Power of Blessing Study Guide

The Power of Imagination

The Power of Imagination Study Guide

The Power of Covenant

The Power of Right Thinking

ABOUT KERRY KIRKWOOD

Kerry Kirkwood is the founding pastor of Trinity Fellowship in Tyler, Texas, founded in 1987. He currently serves as senior pastor and network director of Antioch Oasis International. He helps oversee churches nationally and internationally and is known for his prophetic gifting in prophetic presbytery and conferences. He and his wife, Diane, have four children and six grandchildren.

JOIN *the* CLUB

As a member of the **Love to Read Club,**
receive exclusive offers for FREE, 99¢
and $1.99 e-books* every week. Plus, get
the **latest news** about upcoming releases
from **top authors** like these...

DESTINYIMAGE.COM/FREEBOOKS

**T.D.
JAKES**

**BILL
JOHNSON**

**CINDY
TRIMM**

**JIM
STOVALL**

**BENI
JOHNSON**

**MYLES
MUNROE**